# CONSTRUCTING SUSTAINABLE DEVELOPMENT

# Constructing Sustainable Development

Neil E. Harrison

State University of New York Press

Published by
State University of New York Press

Printed in the United States of America

For information, address State University of New York Press
90 State Street, Suite 700, Albany, NY 12207

Production by Kelli Williams
Marketing by Michael Campochiaro

**Library of Congress Cataloging-in-Publication Data**

Harrison, Neil E., 1949–
    Constructing sustainable development / Neil E. Harrison.
        p. cm.
    Includes bibliographical references and index.
    ISBN 0-7914-4667-0 (alk. paper) — ISBN 0-7914-4668-9 (pbk. : alk paper)
        1. Sustainable development. 2. Social structure. 3. Social values. 4. Social
justice.    I. Title
    HC79.E5 H357 2000
    338.9—dc21                                                          99-058134

10 9 8 7 6 5 4 3 2 1

# CONTENTS

# Acknowledgments

This book grew out of a seminar course that I first taught at the University of Wyoming in the Spring of 1994. Early in that course I discovered that I could not find a satisfactory definition of sustainable development. As the course progressed through reviews of the relevant literature in economics, politics, and environmental ethics, I became progressively more uncertain of what the course was about. Each discipline had something to say, but was clearly biased in its understanding of the issue. Teaching the course again in 1995 and 1998 produced no further answers from the available literature. I have written this book to help me, and I hope the reader, understand what it would take to make development sustainable. My conclusion is quite unlike that offered in any other analysis. This book does not give a recipe for sustainable development. It shows that no recipe is possible. A better metaphor is life itself: perpetual choices in search of the unknown.

I have been aided in this task by a number of people who have read, and sometimes re-read, parts of the manuscript: Gregg Cawley, Rick Green, Fred Homer, James Monke, Tom Princen, and Steve Ropp. All gave me useful advice, some of which I followed; none of them is responsible for any shortcomings that remain. Those I own. I also am grateful to three anonymous reviewers whose insightful comments helped me to tighten up my argument. For their patience, I thank the students who had to suffer as I tried to work out the problem of sustainable development in class. Chapter 4 is a modified version of my article "Why Science and Technology Require Political Guidance to Sustain Development," *Politics and the Life Sciences,* 17, #2 (Fall 1998): 179–188 and is used with permission.

Finally, but most importantly, I thank my wife Ursula for her encouragement and her support against those educational administrators who oppose creativity in the academy. Alex and Kirstie are my hope for the future. May they have the strength to be less materialist and individualist, and more flexible than their parents, but completely themselves.

# 1

## INTRODUCTION

As a growing number of humans each consumes more, the desire for development increasingly conflicts with the environment's ability to provide the services that human society depends on. Through population growth and industrialization, humans made more changes to their natural environment in the twentieth century than in all of prior history (Kates 1994). That trend is not diminishing. Global population is expected to increase from 6 billion today (2000) to about 8.5 billion in 2050, and industrialization continues to invade developing countries (*World Resources 1992–93*, 75–81; Eberstadt 1995). It has been estimated that humanity already appropriates more than 40 percent of the net primary product of terrestrial photosynthesis. A 50 percent increase in population, even without industrialization in less developed countries (LDCs), should increase human consumption of the global available photosynthesis product to about 60 percent (Vitousek et al. 1986).[1]

Industrialization defined the eighteenth century, imperialism the nineteenth century, and the "endless horizon" of science the twentieth century. Sustainable development will become the defining issue of the twenty-first century. Yet, despite its importance, sustainable development is ill defined and poorly understood. A literal interpretation of the term *sustainable development* would be that human development can be continued over the very long term by managing the 'natural,' or nonhuman, environment. The emphasis is on the continuation of development over the very long term, made possible by organizing the environment and the human uses thereof to ensure that goal. Thus, sustainable development is generally understood to mean that human society can continue to develop indefinitely while conserving the natural ecosystems upon which humans rely.[2] It may be defined as: *the balancing of the desire for*

1

*human development and the need to conserve the foundation of natural ecosystems upon which long-term development rests.*

At this level of generality, the concept has become accepted as a " 'metafix' that will unite everybody from profit-minded industrialist and risk-minimizing subsistence farmer to the equity-seeking social worker, the pollution-concerned or wildlife-loving First Worlder, the growth-oriented bureaucrat, and therefore, the vote-counting politician" (Lélé 1991). But what is meant by "human development," "natural," and "eco-systems"? Should ecosystems be conserved, meaning that they can be managed and changed, or should they be preserved? Which ecosystems should be conserved? Individual ecosystems (however defined) or the global ecosystem of which humans are a part, or both? As a general concept, sustainable development is widely accepted; but there is much disagreement about the causes of unsustainability that must be avoided and how sustainable development could be achieved in practice.

THE PROBLEM OF POLICY

Although there is agreement that sustainable development is a worthy goal, there is great contention over which policies will achieve that end. Policies are generally understood as overall plans that guide specific actions by social actors (often governments) to achieve a specified purpose. Thus, they are conscious social action choices designed to create a preferred future state of society.[3] Policies are road maps to desired social futures.

Logically, a problem must be defined before a solution can be crafted, and how the problem is framed selects which policies can offer a solution. Because there is no objective (i.e., scientific) definition of sustainable development—and, as we see in Chapter 2, none is likely—choosing policies implies subjectivity in framing the problem and selecting among alternatives. Without a generally accepted, policy-relevant definition of the problem to be solved, subjective values and beliefs have guided the definition of the problem and the choice of policies.

The interpretation of a broad definition into a policy context reflects certain value judgments. For example, *Our Common Future* (World Commission on Environment and Development 1987) eschews a detailed, policy-relevant definition of sustainable development but identifies "policy directions" that reflect certain social values. The World Commission, also known as the Brundtland Commission, broadly defines sustainable development as "development that meets the needs of the present without compromising the ability of future generations to meet their own needs" (43).

It then argues that "physical sustainability cannot be secured unless development policies pay attention to such considerations as changes in access to resources and in the distribution of costs and benefits." This policy admonition is not an inevitable consequence of its broad conceptualization of sustainable development. The "needs"—however defined—of the present and future may be met in many ways, not only through the material redistribution and political equity policies advocated by that report. Needs may be met by expanding the pie, by carving it up differently, or by changing what humans believe they must have. *Our Common Future* understands needs to be primarily material and satisfied through technology and policies that redistribute the power to control and acquire resources.

Such subjectivity cannot be avoided by attempting a narrow definition of sustainable development. Academic treatises usually attempt to define sustainable development in policy-relevant language before arguing for certain policies (e.g., Pearce et al. 1989; Pearce and Turner 1990; Pearce et al. 1990). However, the choice of definition leads ineluctably to the preferred solution. For example, if sustainable development "involves maximising the net benefits of economic development, subject to maintaining the services and quality of natural resources over time" (Pearce and Turner 1990, 24), policies will logically be designed to enhance economic efficiency and effective environmental management.

If there are insufficient data to frame a problem objectively and substantial dissent over the meaning of the available data, preferred solutions may be used to define the problem (Wildavsky 1979; Dery 1984; Kingdon 1984). Many sustainable development policies have been proposed and some have been implemented (e.g., Carew-Reid et al. 1994; National Commission on the Environment 1993; Sitarz 1993). The definition of the problem may be implied from a detailed discussion of the implementation of the subjectively selected policies. Some recommended sustainable development policies focus on political participation, some on economic efficiency and technology, others on how humans think about their place in creation. Each package of recommended policies implies a different meaning for sustainable development: respectively, a more equitable distribution of power, wealth, and knowledge; a technological adaptation to natural goods limits; and an ideational adaptation to natural goods limits.[4] There is subjectivity in any policy for sustainable development. Whether an attempt is made to translate a broad generally accepted definition into policy-relevant terms or the policy-relevant definition is generated from preferred policies, values and beliefs enter the calculation.[5]

The sustainable development discourse mixes values and beliefs with incomplete data in contending *policy narratives*. Policy narratives are "stories (scenarios and arguments) which underwrite and stabilize the assumptions for policymaking in situations that persist with many unknowns, a high degree of interdependence, and little, if any, agreement" (Roe 1994, 34). They are rhetorical statements about an issue, problematizing it and forming solutions to it out of a cohesive set of beliefs, meanings, understandings, technical concepts, and analytical methods. Narratives "often resist change or modification even in the presence of contradicting empirical data, because they continue to underwrite and stabilize the assumptions for decision making in the face of high uncertainty, complexity, and polarization" (2).

In this book I analyze three dominant sustainable development policy narratives: "efficiency," "equity," and "ethics." Each of these is an argument for a certain set of policies. Based on selected premises, each policy narrative offers conclusions about what policies will lead to sustainable development. I identify the premises and conclusions, and analyze the internal logic of each argument.

Each policy narrative borrows premises and logical arguments from select theories about social and human reality. By using a few assumptions about human behavior, theories build simplified representations or models of reality.[6] Although social science theories are generally designed to explain "what is" (that is, they are positivist), they all also imply "what could be." This book illustrates and critiques each policy narrative by analyzing the theories relevant to the central argument of each narrative. The possible futures implied by each of these theories outline the possibilities for sustainable development. All three narratives assume that sustainable development should be guided by an obligation to permit future generations, at a minimum, development choices comparable to those enjoyed by the present generation. But, they disagree over the meaning of development and over the policies that will sustain it.

## Efficiency

The efficiency narrative is the most common, especially in the industrialized countries. The premise of this narrative is the idea that sustainable development can be achieved by reducing the consumption of natural goods required to maintain or improve human well-being.

An example of the language of this narrative is the description of sustainable development as "an obligation to conduct ourselves so that we leave to the future the option or the capacity to be as well off as we are" (Solow 1993, 181). Similarly, it is allowing the children of the future "to live at least as well as, and preferably better than, people today" (National Commission 1993, 2). In this narrative, increasing "eco-efficiency" reduces pressure on natural goods processes and extends the lives of natural goods stocks.

Eco-efficiency is a measure of the quantity of consumption of natural goods per unit of satisfaction of human needs and wants.[7] It can be increased only through continued economic development, the extension and liberalization of markets (which optimize the efficient allocation of scarce resources), and technological innovation (which enhances productive efficiency and is viewed as a product of markets). Greater wealth is expected to increase eco-efficiency because protection of the environment "has come as a *consequence* of economic development" (Singer 1992, 160). The rate of technological innovation has been enhanced by increased demand for environmental protection and competitive markets. For example, market price signals of the impending depletion of a mineral resource would stimulate technological innovations, increasing the economic viability of marginal ore bodies and creating alternatives. Technological innovation can be expected to increase the rate at which sources are renewed (as through fertilizer or bioengineering) or sink processes operate (through use of bioengineered bacteria to digest wastes).

Chapters 3 and 4 examine the premises and internal logic of the efficiency policy narrative. Chapter 3 examines this internal logic, which (owing much to orthodox microeconomics) holds that free markets will continually increase eco-efficiency and make development sustainable. The chapter concludes that eco-efficiency cannot be assured by markets as understood through microeconomic theory.

The recent evolution of an "ecological economics" offers hope that the underlying concepts of economics will be appropriately adjusted to permit analysis of an economic system that openly interacts with social and natural systems. Based as it is in a macroeconomic conceptualization, this approach emphasizes social goals over pure efficiency, with significant political and policy implications.

Chapter 4 analyzes the problem of producing the technologies necessary to maintain growth in eco-efficiency adequate for sustainable development. Because market-driven technology is undirected, it cannot be relied upon to develop technologies that will automatically succeed in this goal. However, government management of technological systems has been shown to be ineffective. Although sustainable development through technology alone would demand the intrusion of governments into economic and technological systems, optimal technology policies are not immediately apparent. The analysis in chapter 4 suggests a possible alternative to the false dichotomy of command and control and uninhibited markets.

## Equity

This narrative was popularized by the Brundtland Commission and is supported by many United Nations agencies. Commenting that "even a narrow notion of physical sustainability implies a concern for social equity between generations," the Brundtland Commission states as the premise of the equity narrative that "a concern must logically be extended to equity within each generation" (World Commission on Environment and Development 1987, 43). The equity narrative's internal logic reflects this political perspective.

In this narrative, development is a value word that is broader than economists' concepts of "utility" or "wellbeing" (Pearce et al. 1989, 32). It "does not start with goods; it starts with people and their education, organization, and discipline" (Schumacher 1974, 168). It is "a complex series of interrelated change processes, abrupt and gradual, by which a population and all its components move away from patterns of life perceived in some significant way as 'less human' toward alternative patterns of life perceived as 'more human' " (Goulet 1977: x). This is a more elaborate way of saying that the process of development is moving from a "savage nation" to a "civilized and thriving nation" (Smith 1776: I, 1).[8] Similarly, in *Our Common Future,* development is "a progressive transformation of economy *and society.* . . . Physical sustainability cannot be secured unless development policies pay attention to such considerations as changes in *access to resources and in the distribution of costs and benefits*" [emphasis added]; development also meets "the essential needs of the world's poor" (World Commission 1987, 43).[9] In all of these definitions, the development to be sustained includes nonmaterial social order values such as justice and equity.

This is the stuff of politics. Thus, chapters 5 and 6 consider the political problem of predicting and ensuring domestic and international cooperation in pursuit of sustainable development while enhancing social equity. Chapter 5 assesses the possibility of taking communal action without diminishing individual liberty and identifies a model of politics that would help make sustainable development possible. Many authors have suggested that the social cohesion necessary for a large, sustained change in environmental practices demands a reduction in democracy. However, if political participation is a part of sustainable development, as in the equity narrative, handing off responsibility to a technocracy (as suggested by Ophuls and Boyan 1992) is counterproductive.

Chapter 6 considers the need for, and the problem of, international cooperation and concludes that sustainable development is not assured by the current rapid growth in international institutions. Sustainable development can be pursued at the local, national, regional, and global levels. The anarchic international system offers few incentives for cooperation in pursuit of such an imprecise, long-term goal. Chapter 6 assesses the possibility of an effective international response including a substantial change in the political and economic structures that divide the world.

## Ethics

What I call the ethics narrative encompasses a wide variety of radical environmental (or "green") arguments that share a belief in the need for a change in the rules governing the relations between humans and nonhumans. Humans harm the rest of nature because of faults in themselves and their relations within the human community; as Shakespeare wrote: "the fault . . . is not in our stars, but in ourselves" (*Julius Caesar*, I. ii. 134). The premise of the ethics narrative is that sustainable society cannot be achieved without a change in human consciousness.

The rhetoric of this narrative is replete with statements of the need for a transformation in human values and beliefs. For example, sustainable development cannot occur "without a transformation of individual priorities and values. . . . The potential benefits of unleashing the human energy now devoted to producing, advertising, buying, consuming, and discarding material goods are enormous" (Brown et al. 1991). A more extreme statement of the ideas included in this policy narrative is that "it's time for a warrior society to rise up out of the earth and throw itself in front of the juggernaut of destruction, to be antibodies against the human pox that's ravaging this precious, beautiful planet" (Dave Foreman of Earth First! quoted in Gore 1992, 217). If Foreman is not advocating the obliteration of the human species, he is demanding a change in the thoughts and actions that define humanity.

Chapter 7 analyzes the various strands of ecological or green theory that underwrite the ethics narrative. It distinguishes the "dark green" ecological worldview from the more incremental environmental perspective represented by the other two narratives. Grounded in various philosophical or metaphysical arguments about the appropriate relations between humans and nonhumans, green theory cannot easily be translated into practical action. Since all green theories place the primary responsibility for changing consciousness on the individual, decision making is inherently decentralized and large-scale political activity in support of an ecological worldview impractical. The ethics narrative illustrates the importance of ideas in the pursuit of sustainable development.

CONSTRUCTING AN ALTERNATIVE

Sustainable development is a good example of an issue "where the values and interests of opposing camps are so fundamentally divided that no middle ground for compromise exists between them" (Roe 1994, 4). Although each narrative offers valuable insights on this complex issue, none is complete in theoretical analysis or in the policies offered. By analyzing the three policy narratives, this book identifies the strengths and weaknesses of each. The concluding chapter rejects constructing a "metanarrative" (Roe 1994, 4) intended to supersede the three current policy narratives. All three policy narratives (as would a metanarrative) treat sustainable development as a social goal, something to be achieved with the "right" policies, those that are embedded in the narrative.

In the absence of an objective definition (e.g., from science) or a consensual, policy-relevant definition, sustainable development can only be understood as an evolving process in which social and political institutions continuously adapt to changes in scientific knowledge, social values, and ethical concerns. Thus, any narrative—even a metanarrative—that defines a goal would be inappropriate. The concluding chapter suggests a different approach, one derived from modeling human society and its constituent communities as complex systems analogous to living organisms.

By analyzing theories of living or complex systems, chapter 8 derives some principles of sustainable development. These principles should optimize "social adaptive capacity," the ability of human communities to maintain viability in the face of unpredictable changes in their environment. The principles of sustainable development—of living in sustainable human communities—extend and expand the problem definitions and proposed solutions of the three narratives that currently drive discourse. Each policy narrative is a construction of sustainable development from a single point of view, a subjective vision of sustainable development based on selected social values. Each defines sustainable development narrowly in terms of efficiency, equity, or ethics and is only able to offer a simple solution. In the policy narratives, policy for sustainable development becomes a matter of forging a definable social order that is eco-efficient, equitable, or ethical. Modelling humanity and its natural environment as complex adaptive systems generates less subjective principles of policy for sustainable development.

The conclusion argues that sustainable development is a process of continuously adapting to unknown environmental limits and changes. If human society is understood as a complex adaptive system, it constructs sustainable development as a process of survivability through continual adaptation to changes in ecosystems and ideas, institutions, and structures. Humans will construct sustainable development laboriously, policy brick by policy brick, without the benefit of an architectural plan, adapting the design as they learn their needs. Their sole purpose will be to shelter humanity and the rest of life on which humanity depends as best they can within their limited and changing understanding of their world. Despite the absence of a formal design, construction will follow rules that can be derived from understanding human society and its constituent communities as complex adaptive systems. As the conclusion explains, sustainable development is the process of continuously enhancing social adaptive capacity. It is not a place to go; it is a way of traveling.

# 2

# SCIENTIFIC KNOWLEDGE AND UNCERTAINTY

At the core of science lies the belief that 'truth' lies waiting to be discovered with the right scientific method and enough effort. As if, enough digging with the right shovels will uncover sustainable development. A complete scientific assessment of sustainability, whether of local communities, countries, or global society, would require extensive and detailed data about the present and future of natural systems and their interaction, and future human activities and their impact on natural systems. Because the data are insufficient or wholly absent, or are open to various interpretations, science cannot (and probably never will be able to) define sustainable development. Knowledge of sustainability will always be uncertain. This does not imply that scientific research into natural processes is unnecessary; it does mean that science will not play a leading role in defining policy choices. Scientific uncertainty does not prevent policy selection and implementation. But it does mean that the sustainable development discourse will continue to be dominated by ideas (that is, values and beliefs) that construct the problem and its solution.

## MEASURING SUSTAINABILITY

Data on the consumption and availability of sources and sinks are incomplete, uncertain, and the source of contention. Many books have been written attempting to demonstrate that humanity is unconsciously falling into an environmental crisis.[1] Other books have been written rebutting those claims.[2] In large part because scientists have an insufficient understanding of cause/effect relationships to enable them to assess their significance, the available data are inconclusive. There is

11

no consensus about the data nor about their meaning. It is not known—or knowable, at least in scientific terms—if the present development path is sustainable or not. Both those who argue that it is and those who argue that it is not are interpreting raw and inconclusive data through prior beliefs and values.

A few random examples of the incompleteness of the science of source and sink measurement will suffice. Proven reserves of metals range from 38 to 270 years at present rates of consumption, which fluctuate with the business cycle, changes in technology, and prices that are influenced by the availability of alternates.[3] Calculation of the sufficiency of present reserves requires knowledge of the rate of discovery and consumption of ore bodies (which in turn implies knowledge of future technological innovation), the rate of development of practical alternative resources, and the rate and type of economic growth. Similarly, estimates of proven reserves of fossil fuels have remained reasonably steady for forty years despite diminishing numbers of large discoveries ("elephants"), controversies over estimating methods, high and increasing rates of consumption, politically manipulated supplies and prices (e.g., OPEC boycotts), and new technologies (Campbell and Laherrère 1998; Brown 1984; "Major to Minor"). Consumption of fossil energy should continue to increase as the LDCs industrialize (OECD/IEA 1993). According to one estimate, 1 American now uses the same amount of energy as 3 Japanese, 14 Chinese, 168 Bangladeshis, and 531 Ethiopians (Goodland, Daly, and Kellenberg 1992, 149). But depending on the rate of growth of developing economies, and the availability and distribution of energy-saving technologies, it is likely that citizens of developing countries will progressively "learn" Americans' energy consumption habits.

By some measures, food supplies are sufficient; by others, they are insufficient and likely to fall. During the 1980s, grain production increased 24 percent, defeating earlier predictions of global famine (Brown et al. 1995, 26–27; Ehrlich and Ehrlich 1974; Ehrlich 1968). However, there is some evidence that these yield increases came at a cost of diminished soil quality and since 1990 yields have fallen (*World Resources 1994–95*, 84–86, 292; Brown et al. 1995, 25–37; "Will the World Starve?"). Some critics argue that only political failures prevent production of enough food for all the world's growing population (Eberstadt 1995). If predictions of global warming are accurate, yields may fall as pests and crop diseases multiply in a more conducive climate; yet, increases in atmospheric carbon dioxide may increase yields (*World Resources 1994–95*, 108–109; Parry 1990, 37–60; Idso 1989).

In the 1970s, some scientists were predicting global cooling (Ponte 1976; Schneider 1977). Now most scientists believe that "the balance of evidence suggests a discernible human influence on global climate" from anthropogenic emissions of carbon dioxide (Intergovernmental Panel on Climate Change 1995, 22). Great uncertainty remains about the extent and rate of warming, the effects of atmospheric warming on sea levels and local climates, and the effects of climatic changes on natural and socioeconomic systems (Houghton 1994; Intergovernmental Panel on Climate Change 1995). In addition, the scientific community is not united in its interpretation of uncertain scientific data (Balling 1992; Idso 1989; Michaels 1992). On balance, "science still understands little about the world's climate" ("Stay Cool").

Because of a rapid increase in ocean fishing fleets, fish catches in many oceans exceed the estimated sustainable yield, and some fisheries have collapsed (affecting whole ecosystems) or been closed.[4] At the same time, twenty-seven million tons of "unmarketable" species are discarded annually, and mariculture has increased rapidly (Ghazi et al. 1995; *World Resources 1994–95*, 351; "Pollock Overboard"; Brown et al. 1995).

Diversity of species may be essential to a stable ecosystem; elimination of a single species may lead to a fatal imbalance within an ecosystem, with consequences for neighboring systems. However, as only some 1.5 million of the estimated total 8 to 10 million species (some estimates of the total number of species are as high as 100 million) have been documented, estimates of species loss are little more than guesswork. Estimated background or natural rates of species loss are one mammal species every 400 years and one bird species every 200 years. *Known* extinctions total fifty-eight mammals in the last 400 years and 115 bird species in the last 200 years (*World Resources 1994–95*, 148).

This is only a sampling of the myriad controversies about the health of ecosystems and the ability of the environment to provide the sources and sinks necessary for stability and development in human communities. Other problems are of greater concern in individual locales. For example, fresh water is a problem in the Middle East and a factor in the Israel-Palestine conflict (Lowi 1993). Inundation by rising oceans (from global warming) is a concern in small island states and in low-lying coastal states, such as Bangladesh. Food security is a central issue in some LDCs. Toxic waste treatment and air pollution are the primary environmental problems in rich countries.

Environmental problems also interact. For example, deforestation (perhaps to increase the quantity of farmland and, thus, food production) destroys a natural sink for carbon dioxide, reduces the supply of fuel wood for rural peoples, increases soil erosion, and may diminish biodiversity (especially in tropical forests). Because fuel wood is harder to find, people burn an estimated 400 million tons of animal dung, depriving the soil of this natural fertilizer. This in turn reduces global grain yields by 20 million tons, which could feed 100 million people and would be worth $3 billion at 1987 prices (Cairncross 1992, 20). Topsoil loss from unstable hillsides causes other costs such as silting of rivers, which reduces fisheries output, water supplies to urban areas, and hydro-electric production. By the year 2000 the value of the lost energy may have reached as high as $4 billion annually, reducing development in LDCs or increasing fossil fuel demand (*World Resources 1992–93*, 49; Cairncross 1992, 21).

Sustainable development is all of these and many other current environmental problems as well as the interactions between environmental problems, the impacts of development on environment, and the effects of environmental constraints on human development far into the future. Because we know little about the limits of individual sources and sinks and the dangers to human communities and constraints on their development of exceeding those limits, we cannot comprehend sustainable development—as the sum of all relations between human and nonhuman systems—through science. As Robert D. Mahlman, Director of the Geophysical Fluid Dynamic Laboratory (U.S.), commented about climate change (but it applies equally well to sustainable development): "The things we can say with confidence, the policy makers are not interested in. And the things [they] are interested in, we don't know with confidence" (White 1990, 41). Science can never tell us what we should do; at best it will be able to identify the ecological effects of certain specific local actions, or of inaction.

Science cannot define the limits intrinsic in natural systems and is unable to predict how human systems would be affected by exceeding them. Experts can make guesses, but they are a long way from useful, policy-relevant, scientific knowledge. In part, this is because the methods of orthodox science are ill adapted to studying the relatedness and wholeness of natural systems. Reductionist methods test a hypothesized cause-effect relationship by isolating it from all other influences. Where complete isolation of the cause-and-effect elements of systems is impossible, as often in the life sciences and the social sciences, this approach is less effective. This methodology contrasts with newer scientific theories such as quantum mechanics, chaos, and complexity, which suggest that prediction of outcomes in even simple systems is impossible (Gleick 1987; Waldrop 1992). Finally, scientific disciplines disagree on relevant assumptions, on what is the important object of study, on methods, and on what constitutes scientific evidence (Keyfitz 1995). The paucity of reliable scientific data, the poor understanding of interactions between ecosystems and their constituent parts, and the methodology of science itself conspire to ensure scientific uncertainty.

Not only is science uncertain, it will continue to be so for the foreseeable future. In order to define sustainable development in scientific terms science would have to, at a minimum:

1. Understand natural ecosystems and their interactions so that the effects of human invasion are predictable.

2. Quantify these predictions for specific sources and sinks and be able to aggregate them to predict overall environmental vulnerability to human incursions. This requires quantified predictions for the human effect on individual sources and sinks *and* on the natural systems in which they are embedded.

3. Predict the rate and type of human consumption of natural sources and natural sinks. This requires prediction of the level and type of economic activity.

4. Predict future population and future technological innovations.

5. Predict the tastes and choices of future generations that will affect economic activity and social structures.

THE ROLE OF UNCERTAINTY

Uncertainty is the "certainty that one of several outcomes will occur; but which one is unknown and *unknowable*" (Chacko 1991, 5; emphasis added). Risk, a concept commonly used in environmental issues to aid in policy analysis, is a function of the expected damage or loss from an event and the probability of that event occurring. It "describes the situations where the exact outcome is not known but the outcome does not represent a novelty. Uncertainty applies to cases where the reason why we cannot predict the outcome is that the same event has never been observed in the past, and, hence, it may involve a novelty" (Georgescu-Roegen 1971, 122). *Novelty* means that there is no history of comparable events from which to predict future events, either directly or by hypothesizing cause-effect relations. Sustainable development encompasses so many natural and social issues that even when treated discretely they do not yet (and may never) permit us sufficient knowledge to form an understanding of cause-effect relations with which to assign objective probabilities to outcomes. Taken collectively, we will probably never be able to predict the outcome of specific actions designed to sustain development.

Decision rules under uncertainty generally require the use of both empirical data and subjective probabilities to assess the probability of an event occurring. Given a subjective preference ordering of outcome utilities, knowledge both of the consequences of actions and the probability of those consequences occurring makes rational calculation relatively mechanical. Subjective probabilities can be constructed based on incomplete evidence of relationships between variables, or on a knowledge or understanding of the causal relations linking events. Recurring, comparable events refine subjective probabilities. Considering sustainable development, neither the outcomes of actions nor the probability of their occurrence can be objectively determined, and the problem as a whole is a novelty. Both outcomes and probabilities must be assessed subjectively. Nevertheless, it is still rational to maximize expected utility even when this must be calculated with a subjective preference ordering and a subjective assessment of the nature and probability of outcomes.[5] Thus, the absence of *objective* evidence that development is at present unsustainable does not mean that the problem of sustainable development should not be considered in depth.

Rational choice under uncertainty becomes a choice of worst or best possible outcomes depending on risk aversion or acceptance. Risk-averse individuals will choose to avoid the worst case; more risk-accepting individuals will hope for the best (Elster 1986). The best case would be that business-as-usual is sustainable over the long term. Social systems would naturally evolve to maintain balance between the demand and supply of essential natural goods. The worst case is that only substantial social change will avert a collapse of the ecological support of human society. Because sustainable development is uncertain, the choice is between (1) incurring present social and economic costs in anticipation of a worst-case scenario, and (2) hoping for the best. For the first choice, possible outcomes are that these efforts will avert a crisis and that resources will be expended unnecessarily.[6] For the second choice, possible outcomes are social catastrophe and avoidance of the social and economic costs of unnecessary mitigation. The precautionary principle (popular with environmentalists) that scientific uncertainty should not be used to justify an absence of responsive policy and that a reasonable presumption of harm is enough to attempt to mitigate a possible undesirable environmental change, reflects risk aversion. Reliance on science to define mitigative policies and actions to sustain development is more risk accepting.

Although individual subjective probabilities may approximate guesswork, a common solution is to combine expert opinions of a subjective probability to improve reliability. Still, because sustainable development is mostly about the behavior of human groups, personal preferences for social outcomes and orders intrude into purportedly disinterested statements (Diesing 1982 and 1991). Differing preferences for future social orders are part of the contention over policy choices in the context of scientific uncertainty. For example, elites who have benefitted from the present social order will be more accepting of business-as-usual even if it can be shown that this is a more risk-accepting strategy.

Because of a paradox within it, sustainable development becomes socially constructed. If scientific uncertainty should not inhibit responsive policy, policy is necessary. But scientific knowledge cannot define a policy path to sustainable development. Thus, sustainable development becomes socially constructed; it is presently framed within a discourse between policy narratives that assume different social values and beliefs. Because of differences in their premises, each policy narrative frames the problem differently and offers a different construction of the solution. Each assumes the precautionary principle; none specifically rejects science, but none embraces it.

Sustainable development is a problem of collectivities (villages, cities, nations, etc.), a problem so extensive and affecting so many individuals and groups that it demands collective action. A collective preference ordering of outcomes and a collective assessment of the probabilities of policy outcomes combine to create an expected utility of collective action (i.e., policies). Policy narratives help collectivities to construct an image of sustainable development (i.e., policy outcomes) and to choose policies for achieving this imagined world. Each policy narrative favors a different social mechanism for reaching a collective expected utility. Collective expected utility may be achieved through market systems as discussed in chapter 3, through political systems as discussed in chapter 5, or through the propagation of a common ideology as suggested in chapter 7.

# 3

## THE EFFICIENCY NARRATIVE:
## ECO-EFFICIENCY THROUGH MARKETS

The efficiency narrative argues that the key to sustainable development is an economy that adapts to ecological limits as they are identified by progressively increasing eco-efficiency. Technological innovation increases the efficiency with which natural goods are used in satisfying human wants (Rosenberg 1994; Rosenberg and Birdzell 1990; "The Price of Light"). Many economists now believe that technological innovation rather than Smithian allocative efficiency also plays the major role in economic development and wealth production (Romer 1986; Solow 1957, 312–320; Hill 1979). It seems likely that "a sustained high rate of growth depends upon the continuous emergence of new inventions and innovations" (Kuznets, quoted in Rosenberg 1982, 258). Historically, the market has been very effective at producing technological change. Thus, the premise of the efficiency narrative is explained by Singer (1992, 160): "technology and the right political system—these are indeed the necessary and perhaps even the sufficient ingredients of sustainable development." The "right" political system minimizes external interference in the operation of the market.

Because of the importance of efficiency and, thus, of the market in this narrative, the language of economics dominates its rhetoric. The triumph of the neoclassical paradigm is reflected in the persistent application of the market metaphor to nearly every economic and social problem. As Nobel Laureate Gary Becker has written, neatly summarizing the principles of neoclassical economics, "combined assumptions of maximising [individual] behavior, market equilibrium and stable preferences, used relentlessly and unflinchingly, form the heart of the economic approach as I see it. . . . The economic approach is a comprehensive one that is applicable to all human behavior" (quoted in Hodgson 1994, 23).

19

However, this chapter shows that the market as modeled by economic orthodoxy cannot reduce the human consumption of natural goods sufficiently to sustain development.[1] A nascent alternative "ecological economics" appropriately views the economic system as interacting with social and natural systems but is not yet adequately developed to be a useful framework for policymaking. The next chapter shows that leaving selection of technological innovation to the market will not ensure that eco-efficiency increases. However, political direction of technological innovation is problematic.

AN ORTHODOX VIEW

The goal of neoclassical economics is to explain how to allocate scarce resources in order to satisfy the unlimited wants of consumers. Neoclassical economics describes the economy in microeconomic terms as the sum of the individual decisions of producers and consumers through markets, generally ignoring non-economic factors and actors. Through prices, a scarce supply of resources is allocated to the demand for goods and services in a static economy. Welfare economics historically has been rooted in the desire of many economists to maintain contact between theoretical analysis and socially relevant themes. But under the neoclassical influence, the "perspective has shifted from some general utility for society as a whole to the separate utilities of single individuals which cannot be aggregated into a societal sum-total. . . . Statements on total utility and similar matters should therefore be avoided in scientific research since they are bare of 'scientific content' " (Rothschild 1993, 58). In neoclassical economics, social utility is the aggregation of individual utilities, each the result of subjective individual preferences. In contrast, classical economists such as Smith (1776) were concerned with the long-run development of whole economies.

The hegemony of neoclassical thought means that "two elements occupy a central place in modern welfare economics: the notion of Pareto-optimality and the role of perfect markets in connection with Pareto-optimality" (Rothschild 1993, 65–66). As a consequence, interpersonal comparisons of utility are considered inappropriate and "the partly psychological, partly 'ethical' idea that additional material wealth will increase individual utility and that increases in utility are a desirable target" is assumed. Thus arises the "normative pro-market stance" of neoclassical economics in which individual utility may best be increased through economic growth, itself maximized through efficiency.

By the late nineteenth century, economists were able to show that no government interference in the market was justified as it would regulate itself (Heilbroner 1980, 168–209). The free-market auction between self-interested buyers and sellers will reach an efficient equilibrium price of its own accord and the market will clear. In the very short run, this market clearing price will be most influenced by demand; but in a competitive market over the longer run, the price will tend toward the cost of production.

Two centuries of theoretical and empirical analysis seem to support the view that the neoclassical model is a reasonably accurate representation of the reality of markets and that markets optimize efficiency. Thus, markets are central to the efficiency narrative, and its language is that of neoclassical or "orthodox" economics. This chapter analyzes six ways in which markets as modelled by orthodox economics may not sustain development. First, markets tend to encourage consumption and externalities. Second, markets cannot trade most natural goods without government intervention that contradicts the freedom ethic of the market. Third, because individual needs and preferences may not coincide with optimal social or natural rates of resource depletion, consumption of natural resources may not be optimized by allocation of private property rights in resources. Fourth, while privatization of natural resources is expected to improve the efficiency of their consumption, similar mechanisms are generally ineffective for restricting the use of natural sinks. Fifth, if markets are relatively static, tending to equilibrium (as the orthodox model describes them), they do not reflect the dynamic character of social and natural systems. Finally, the market's emphasis on individual freedom is in stark contrast with the collective nature of the problem of sustainable development. If sustainable development is a problem, it is a collective problem requiring a collective response. An exclusive concern for individual choices is not helpful.

A separate section discusses a macroeconomic perspective that diverges in important respects from neoclassical orthodoxy. Ecological economics' emphasis on systemic relations between economic, natural, and social systems reduces the importance of markets. A concluding section discusses how markets might be directed to help sustain development.

MARKETS AND CONSUMPTION

The consumption of natural goods could be minimized by reducing consumer demand for goods and services. Classical economists expected that once needs (that each human *must* have) had been satisfied, the rate of increase in demand would slow. Neoclassical economics assumes that consumers have no internal restrictions on wants. If this is a reasonable assumption, the market may be the ideal mechanism for most efficiently satisfying the ever-expanding individual wants of a myriad of self-regarding consumers but at the expense of sustainable development. The relatively greater growth and productivity of market economies over centrally controlled economies suggests that the hidden hand of prices coordinates producer and consumer decisions more effectively than human agency. Any external restriction on human wants would reduce personal liberty, while development is often viewed as a path of increasing personal liberty.[2] Thus, reflecting the value preferences of the neo-classical project, in the efficiency narrative development is understood as the continuous expansion of the means to satisfy material human wants while preserving individual freedom of material choice and of use of property.[3] In recent years this goal of economic activity has become ever more widely espoused; the prescribed policy is to free markets from political interference.

Absent increases in productive efficiency (discussed in chapter 4), natural goods consumption within a free market economy can only be reduced by consumers demanding fewer material goods. Two factors make this unlikely. First, producers are rewarded for encouraging consumption. Second, to the extent that consumers use material goods to construct their identity and identity is relative to others, the demand for material consumption may be infinite.

If "wants multiply with the multiplication of the means to satisfy them" (Levine 1995, 20), product differentiation encourages consumption. Wants are general; they are for food, transportation, leisure, and so on. Individually, consumers may interpret these wants as lobster or linguine, automobiles or aircraft, and hang-gliding or hiking. Although we assume that consumers form their wants independently, producers influence consumer preferences through advertising, product differentiation, and market segmentation. Through such practices of profit-seeking firms, the competitive market raises the priority of those preferences that may be satisfied through the market.[4]

Material goods also may be a means to social esteem.[5] Material goods may be used not only to satisfy material needs but also psychological needs and wants (if only temporarily), or to construct an image of the self in relation to others (Levine 1995, 20–33; 1988). Fashion is a means of projecting an image, either of belonging (teen hip-hop fashions) or of distinction (Dior dresses). In that sense, material wants may be relational rather than absolute. What utility is a car like a Ferrari that can exceed the legal speed limit by 100 miles per hour if it does not satisfy some nonmaterial needs? Positional goods, such as education or a house with large grounds and a unique view, are valuable because they confer special status on their owner (Hirsch 1976). Wealth in the mere millions is insufficient to win public awe; now, only billions are wondrous. In 1995, Warren Buffet had a net worth of about $16 billion (Greenwald 1995). Seeing wealth as a way of "keeping score," he intended to continue to grow his wealth, and he has.

Daly (1993) argues that reducing income inequalities would decrease competitive pressures for economic growth. Because the market rewards participants in accordance with their ability to satisfy the demands of others, "everybody is paid according to his [economic] contribution" (Von Mises, quoted in Rothschild 1993, 47). Thus, the demand for relative economic position may be an essential requirement of market economies (Okun 1975; Daly and Cobb 1989, 87–88; "For Richer, For Poorer").[6] Markets will not result in the income distribution that would minimize competitive acquisition.

Only if consumption patterns change can the market contribute directly to sustainable development. A "greening" of consumption is not likely to be instigated by firms (but, for example, see Schmidheiny 1992). Any change in consumer preferences that would reduce material consumption will be the result of activities exogenous to the market. For example, if consumers understood material goods as "things that flow on through," rather than "as things that are stored and possessed" (Schmookler 1993, 57; Locke 1980), consumption might be restrained. The market for environmental services (including education of consumers) provided by environmental nongovernment organizations (ENGOs) has affected public awareness of environmental issues and personal consumer preferences.[7] Arguments that the greening of consumption will sufficiently reduce demand and, therefore, that markets can directly sustain development, are unsupported by empirical evidence. Such arguments reflect a preference for the sanctity of freedom of choice, for those with property, in the acquisition and use of that property.

## EXCLUSION OF NATURAL GOODS

The market efficiently allocates only those goods that it recognizes: goods and services subject to private property rights. Enforceable private property rights, the protection of which is a primary government responsibility, make markets possible (Nozick 1974; Friedman 1962). Markets "fail" when property rights cannot be adequately defined or enforced. With respect to sustainable development, markets fail to provide collective goods[8] and encourage overuse of open access sources and sinks.[9]

Any form of publicness or open access encourages overuse of limited resources; private ownership is expected to encourage efficient use. Common pool resources[10] are limited stocks (such as an oil reservoir) or flows (such as grass) of natural goods which it is, in practice, difficult to exclude individuals from use and benefit (Ostrom et al. 1994).[11] In the absence of social restraints on the access to or use of the common pool resource, rational economic persons seek to capture all the benefit of its use while bearing a minimal cost, usually resulting in its overuse and destruction.[12]

Privatization is the preferred solution of neoclassical economists to problems of common pool resources. By assigning property rights to the resource, its product can be traded in the market. Common examples are the forest products and oil found on public land. Similarly, governments encourage the private production of what would otherwise be public goods by allowing those who produce them to enjoy an exclusive benefit. For example, new knowledge is privatized through the patent system.

There are many ways to privatize natural resources, including ownership of the resource, as in mineral rights; assigning tradeable quotas, for example, for access to fishing grounds; and granting long-term leases, as in grazing rights on public lands. In each case, it is presumed that private owners will be concerned with the efficient management of the resource. Through optimal mining, fishing, or grazing practices, stock resources will be consumed most efficiently and flow resources will be managed to maintain the highest possible level of production over time. As the next section argues, this presumption is often misleading.

Because they lack a market value, the consumption of many natural goods is omitted from gross domestic product (GDP, a measure of aggregate economic activity within national borders) deceiving business leaders and policymakers about the true state of national finances. The rate of economic growth is overstated and macroeconomic decision making distorted. By only measuring economic activity through market transactions, "motoring . . . raises GNP more than bicycling; stoking the furnace adds more than wearing a sweater" (Goodland and Daly 1992a), and waste of resource and production of waste is "beneficial." Activities that damage sinks become a "good" through inclusion of remediation and health costs in GDP. The Exxon Valdez oil spill increased GDP. Including measures of resource depletion can result in substantial reductions in GDP ("Wealth of Nature"; "Costa Nature"). One calculation of an alternative measure of U.S. social welfare, an Index of Sustainable Economic Welfare, shows increases in the 1960s and 1970s and a *decline* in the 1980s (Daly and Cobb 1989, 401–455).

Bringing all natural goods into the market would require government intervention. From the point of view of neoclassical economics this is the primary role of government (for example, Friedman 1962; Hayek 1994). However, economists underestimate the political difficulty of granting a minority of individuals the right to control access to important natural resources now publicly held, especially in a society that seeks to maintain social cohesion through a degree of equity.[13] If restricting use of public lands exacerbates wealth inequities, this may have serious social consequences and may encourage overconsumption (Daly 1993).

## PROBLEMS WITH PRIVATE EXPLOITATION

Neoclassical orthodoxy assumes that individual owners of natural resources will deplete their resource property at a rate that ensures efficient allocation of consumption over time. To achieve this they will include in total cost a notional scarcity rent, a form of marginal user cost that reflects the opportunity cost of current production (future income foregone). The scarcity rent is a function of the present value of the resource, which is dependent on the discount rate and knowledge of future resource prices.[14] Under rationality assumptions knowledge of future market prices still requires knowledge of (1) the stock of resource available globally; (2) the demand over time for the resource; (3) the technically optimal rate of production (which may change with technological innovation); and (4) the substitutability between resources over time.

Dynamic efficiency is maximized when the present values of the marginal net benefits of all time periods are equal, and there is no incentive to move some of the resources from one period to another (Tietenberg 1994, 25). In addition to calculating scarcity rent, to optimize dynamic efficiency, resource owners must appropriately discount future income flows. Thus, both scarcity rent and dynamic efficiency are sensitive to choices of discount rate. Although "when people have ownership rights in resources, there is a stronger incentive to protect the value of those resources" (DiLorenzo 1993), private owners of natural goods may not consume them at a rate that is privately, socially, or ecologically optimal.

Private decisions on resource exploitation rates are based on private needs, including but not limited to interperiod dynamic efficiency. Resource owners have concerns in the present that influence decision making about the rate of extraction. These include cash flow and profits (especially if the owner is a firm whose stock is publicly traded), maintenance of employment and market share, full employment of fixed assets, and so on. In practice, cash flow demands often dictate the rate of exploitation, in part because accounting costs do not include opportunity costs. Hard-headed businesswomen rarely base production decisions on

guesses about the long-term future. For example, although total estimated reserves have fallen or remained flat, and the total portion of
liquid hydrocarbons (including natural gas) remaining in the earth's
surface is obviously diminishing, the price of oil has fallen since 1981
rather than risen. By early 1999 it was lower in real terms than in the
early 1970s but then more than doubled in nine months. Factors other
than the scarcity of the resource and the cost of recovery have influenced
its price. Political considerations including United Nations' sanctions on
Iraq and Saudi Arabia's security relations with the United States as well
as the latter's ability to maintain its cash flow in the face of prices that
are declining as a result of non-OPEC production have influenced oil
production rates and prices. Technical limits on the rate of sustainable
production from a geological structure also must be observed in order to
optimize total production.[15]

Private discount rates (a measure of the subjective time value of
money) are usually assumed to reflect the cost of money together with
a risk premium that compensates for factors such as legislative uncertainties (Tietenberg 1994, 43). Ideally, private discount rates would equal
the social discount rate, that discount rate that would allocate the resource across generations most efficiently for the society. Yet, for many
reasons, private producers often have higher discount rates than would
be necessary for a socially efficient allocation of resources between generations. For example, although energy-saving products such as compact
fluorescent lightbulbs have a higher capital cost, most repay that cost in
energy savings within less than two years. However, consumers who
would balk at borrowing at 20 percent reject a rate of return on investment of more than 40 percent from such products.[16]

Social discount rates are affected by many economic and social
factors. For example, a social preference for low unemployment or low
inflation will affect the social cost of money, as will growth in demand,
changes in trade balances, and so on. A high social discount rate allocates scarce financial resources most efficiently, but screens out projects
with lower annual returns over a longer period (such as energy conservation or education programs) that might be a part of sustainable development. Lowering discount rates to ensure that such projects are included
would require subsidization of the cost of money and would leave the
private resource owner with a large number of alternate uses of capital,
many of which may have comparable returns with no clear choice on
this criterion alone. Negative real interest rates (that is, subsidized by
governments) misallocate resources in the present and are thought to
impede economic development ("Economic Miracle or Myth?").
Sustainability cannot be achieved merely by fiddling discount rates to

reflect social time preferences. The problem of interest rates points to the need explicitly to consider intergenerational equity (Arndt 1993). Solow, a Nobel Laureate, comments (1986): "One's strongest impression is that we have very little to go on in the making of decisions with very long-run consequences. . . . The tendency is very great to allow short-run considerations to dominate, if only because we can grasp them better."[17] Unless private resources owners take into account ecological considerations such as maintaining the flow of natural goods or extending stock lives, they will probably consume their assets at a rate that is higher than socially optimal.

## REGULATING NATURAL SINKS

Externalities occur when a production operation causes others to bear a portion of the full social cost of production.[18] Thus, an externality is the cost-free consumption of a sink by a producer. As privatization of sinks is often impractical,[19] consumption of sinks is reduced through regulation of externalities. Externalities will be reduced (and open-access sinks retained) if polluters are motivated to include the full social cost of production in the cost of their products.

Coase (1960) has shown that under most conditions, social efficiency can be maximized whether producers pay to avoid the harm or victims bear the cost of the harm or its remediation.[20] For local sink consumption this may be possible. Acidification of a lake by deposition from a smokestack may impose a small social cost on local people; if the social cost is too great it is possible to reverse the acidification process. However, this approach ignores the possibility of ecological limits to sinks and nonlinear responses when sinks are close to capacity.[21] In either case, the social cost of the pollution may be substantially greater than the economic cost of pollution avoidance. Also, depletion of the ozone layer through CFC emissions or warming of the atmosphere from carbon dioxide emissions cannot be remedied directly with available technology. In some countries, the cost of the social dislocation required to adapt to climate change may greatly exceed the cost of mitigation measures.[22] Also, social costs incurred from unremediated open access to sinks may include loss of natural goods and services that are not tradeable, such as intangible existence values and other psychological benefits. Thus, despite Coase's elegant economic analysis, development is more likely to be sustained through the re-engineering of production to reduce sink consumption than by remediation of sink damage.

Governments can encourage producers to minimize externalities through direct regulation or through market mechanisms that allocate a cost for use of open-access sinks. More economically efficient use-cost alternatives include a tax on polluting inputs (such as a tax on the carbon content of fuels), license fees, and tradeable pollution permits. Tradeable pollution permits can be criticized as unjust because they permit wealthier polluters to avoid reducing pollution, or as morally abhorrent because they effectively assign private property rights to a portion of a sink. A more serious criticism is that, unless the total permitted emissions are progressively reduced, they institutionalize pollution rather than encourage re-engineering of production (Cairncross 1989).

To minimize drag on the economy, government intervention must reflect the actual social cost of each externality. However, techniques for calculating social cost are imprecise. The most popular technique, contingent valuation, attempts to quantify the value in monetary terms that citizens place on specific environmental goods.[23] Contingent valuation has been criticized on a number of counts: that it is unrealistic; that it does not measure citizen's values; and that citizens may reject the concept of trading "dollars for pollution 'rights'," thus invalidating the results (Sagoff 1988; Stirling 1993; "The Price of Imagining Arden"). Proposals to improve the quality of contingent valuation, including making the choice more realistic and asking closed-ended rather than open-ended questions about the price the respondent is willing to pay, might improve its accuracy. Still, even if social preferences could be quantified and included in natural goods prices, there is no assurance that the amount respondents are willing to pay would be sufficient to prevent sink damage.

MARKET MECHANICS

Robbins has called economics "the *science* which studies human behavior as a relationship between ends and scarce means which have alternative uses" (quoted in Rothschild 1993, 58; emphasis added). Through selective assumptions, human behaviors become sufficiently consistent that neoclassical economics could be assumed to deal with "quantities [that] could be translated into mathematics" (Heilbroner 1980, 170–173). In pursuit of a scientific and mathematical methodology for understanding social phenomena, neoclassical economics assumes that humans are rational in their pursuit of self-interest, understood as the satisfaction of unlimited material wants that are determined outside the market.[24]

Although consumers confuse changes in money prices with changes in real prices (misunderstanding the effects of inflation) and give in to temptations of the moment, therefore saving less than economists predict they should, economists defend the assumptions necessary to mathematically model behavior. It can be argued, as Friedman has, that assuming that an expert billiard player knows the mechanical formulae for her shots is reasonable even if she never studied mathematics: her behavior accords with the formulae most of the time.

Although "the assumption of rationality makes theorising a cinch," the models too often do not accord with reality (Brian Arthur quoted in "Rational Economic Man"). Orthodox economics assumes that individuals have "vast deductive capabilities when in fact they operate inductively using rules of thumb to guide behavior." Recall the problem of the owner of a natural resource calculating the scarcity rent of his asset. Abstractions from human reality, necessary for mathematical methodological rigor, lead to the "fallacy of misplaced concreteness" (Daly and Cobb 1989, 35–36) and "unwarranted conclusions about concrete actuality" (Georgescu-Roegen 1971, 320).

The greatest ambition of the founders of the neoclassical school was "to build an economic science after the model of mechanics—in the words of W. Stanley Jevons—as *'the mechanics of utility and self-interest'* " (Georgescu-Roegen 1975). But if the economic process is viewed as a "mechanical analogue consisting—as all mechanical analogues do—of a principle of conservation (transformation) and a maximization rule," its central tenets would lead us to expect that the economy will never reach the point of destroying the environment; it can always withdraw from the brink. Neoclassical economics' "fatally simple structure imposed on it in the eighteenth century" has made it "deterministic, predictable and mechanistic" (Arthur 1990). In reality the economy is "complex . . . process-dependent, organic and always evolving."[25] Sustainable development should be viewed as the result of cumulative processes (thus, requiring study of those processes). Neither social nor economic systems are adequately modeled as a pendulum always returning to equilibrium: "the economic process like any other life process, is irreversible" (Georgescu-Roegen, 1975). Nature is dynamic; ecosystems are never in balance, they are in dynamic equilibrium that can fall off into radical metamorphosis because of a minor change in a small part of the system. No mechanical analog can model the interaction of the life processes, of human society and ecosystems. A more appropriate model borrowed from the life sciences would emphasize dynamic processes over static equilibrium and would be less determinate.

## MARKETS AND COLLECTIVE RESPONSE

The market of neoclassical economics focuses on efficiently satisfying individual wants with scarce resources: market choice is the accumulation of myriad individual choices. But as a problem of the development of human society, sustainable development is a collective problem. As Arrow (1951) has pointed out, aggregation of individual preferences may not result in a social preference ordering that is either supported by the majority or technically optimal.

Although some environmentalists have argued that, with appropriate information, consumers can make market choices that satisfy not only their material wants but their desire for reduced environmental harm (Brown 1991), the market has "no organs for hearing, feeling, or smelling either justice or sustainability" (Daly and Cobb 1989, 146). Can the consumer demand food that is grown sustainably when large intermediary corporations choose between a large number of suppliers on the basis of price and quality, not growing methods?

As a collective problem, sustainable development demands policies that respond to the quantity, type, and ecological impacts of aggregate economic activity. If priority is given to creating a balance between the economy, with social needs collectively determined, and the limits of ecosystems, the efficiency of markets can be directed, reducing human consumption of natural goods. Ecological economics, reviewed in the next section, is 'environmental macroeconomics' that subordinates the market to social goals such as sustainable development or environmental preservation.

## ECOLOGICAL ECONOMICS

The assumption of ecological limits challenges many of the premises of economic orthodoxy.[26] Because "economics has been keen to translate any notion of 'economic improvement' into a variable to be measured and compared" (Barbier 1987, 101), it has pursued a predictive understanding of the processes of the economic system by assuming away the "necessary" interaction of the economy and the environment (Pearce et al. 1989, xiv). Ecological economics attempts to rectify that error by treating the economic system as open to social and ecological systems. In ecological economics, the consumer is only "one component (albeit a very important one) in the overall system" in which the economy co-evolves with other technological, political, and ecological systems (Costanza et al. 1991). It uses an ecology analog to model the interaction of production and consumption processes with social and ecosystem processes.

Ecological economics links macroeconomics with ecology and draws a distinction between the optimal allocation of resources and the optimal scale of economic activity, a legitimate but ignored objective of

**Table 1**

Comparing Orthodox Economics, Ecology, and Ecological Economics

|  | Orthodox Economics | Ecology | Ecological Economics |
|---|---|---|---|
| Basic world view | Mechanistic, usually static, atomistic | Evolutionary, atomistic | Dynamic, systems evolutionary |
| Time frame | Short (to 50 years) | Multiscale | Multiscale |
| Space frame | Local to international | Local to regional | Local to global |
| Species frame | Humans only | Nonhumans only | Whole ecosystems, including humans |
| Primary macro goal | Growth of national economy | Survival of species | Economic system sustainability |
| Primary micro goal | Maximum profits, maximum utility | Maximum reproductive success | Adjusts to reflect system goals |
| Technology assumptions | Very optimistic | Pessimistic or no opinion | Prudently skeptical |
| Academic stance | Disciplinary | Disciplinary | Transdisciplinary |

*Adapted from Costanza et al. 1991, 5.*

macroeconomic policy. It recognizes that the economy—a dynamic system of production, exchange, and consumption—is open to and interacts with the natural ecosystem and the social system. As shown in Table 1, ecological economics has many similarities to ecology and differencies from orthodox economics.

"Steady-state economics" is an early example of ecological economics. It proposes four macro social goals: a constant human population; a constant stock of artifacts; the levels at which population and stock are held constant is sufficient for "a good life and sustainable for a long future"; and the rate of throughput of matter-energy is at the lowest feasible level (Daly 1993, 325). These goals connect the economy to the broader society and the natural environment. Social institutions would reduce disparities of wealth and would limit the growth of population and of the use of natural resources, with the goal of limiting the scale of the economy to a level consistent with ecosystem health. Development would continue through increasing eco-efficiency by aiming technological innovation (the subject of chapter 4) at the problem of efficient use of resources rather than efficient satisfaction of wants, and the substitution of renewable for nonrenewable resources.

Daly argues that an institutional cap on maximum wealth and per capita income and support of minimum income would limit competitive accumulation and rectify distortions in property rights endemic in modern industrialized societies. Locke proposed that individuals would not accumulate more property by mixing their labor with land than was necessary for their own support: property is only "relative to human need" and should be "acquired through personal effort" (McCluaghry, quoted in Daly 1993, 333–334). Once this idea of sufficiency is institutionalized, together with limits on corporate size, strikes could be outlawed and unions abolished, and large quantities of savings seeking large returns would be unnecessary. Thus would much of the pressure for economic growth be eliminated. However, Locke himself argued that once the market is available, such self-restraint would end and government would be required; the market permits land to be acquired by money and stored (Locke 1980, 28, 57).

Transferable birth licenses could limit population growth. As these licenses grow in value they could be another means of equalizing wealth: poorer owners (probably women) could sell them to richer persons who seek larger families. Daly recognizes the abhorrence most people would feel at this limitation and marketization of what most consider an adult woman's right. He argues that it is necessary, rational, and moral. It is "not the exchange relationship that debases life . . . it is the underlying inequity in wealth and income beyond any functional or ethical justification" that makes us automatically seek to reject it (Daly 1993, 339).

Daly also recommends an institution to prevent excessive exploitation of natural resources through depletion quotas that restrict the right of resource owners to produce from their property. Quotas are preferred to taxes as the most direct means of limiting resource use by ensuring that an appropriate scarcity rent is included in resource prices.

Daly designed these institutions to severely limit the level of interaction of the economy with the natural ecosystem and to solve the problem of the proper scale of the economy. However, the goal of reducing the entropic production of the economy is achieved at the cost of extensive intervention in the market, with presumed losses of economic efficiency.

Ecological economics still pursues formal models and quantitative methods. As in neoclassical theory, development is assumed to be limited to material production, and the institutions that Daly describes suggest political structures that imply a retrogression in human and social development. The more equal distribution of wealth deemed necessary to restrain consumption is a poor substitute for justice or equality, and reproduction limits restrict human rights. As Ophuls and Boyan (1992) argues, the transition to the steady state might require authoritarian rule, an issue taken up in chapter 5. Also, for the steady state to sustain development it must be steady at a sustainable level, which, as chapter 2 argued, cannot be objectively determined.

Ecological economics remains limited by many of the concepts and methods of orthodox economics. In neoclassical economics, the objective is to maximize the net benefit of all inputs to production (land, labor, and physical capital). In contrast, ecological economics argues that the appropriate objective is to maximize the present value of natural capital, and especially of scarce, nonrenewable resources. Future generations might be compensated for consumption of natural capital through "a system of effluent charges, environmental rental charges, and lump sum transfers" such that "different generations realize the same level of equity" (Becker 1982). Some trade-off of physical or human capital for natural capital might be permitted and would be necessary.

The orthodox view offers "weak" sustainability that allows replacement of all natural capital with human or physical capital.[27] Tongue in cheek, Garrison Keillor (1995) gives us a glimpse of the future under weak sustainability. He suggests that Minnesota might want to consider selling the fresh water from Lake Superior and its in-state lakes to the desert Southwest and West. The colossal income from this sale would attract so many people to Minnesota that New York and other major commercial centers would shut down. Once Lake Superior is drained (by 2020) the now largest canyon in the world would attract huge numbers of tourists. With the income from the sale of water, the canyon floor could be filled with offices, factories, and hotels.

The "strong" sustainability of ecological economic would privilege natural capital; but it, too, is problematic. For example, "much environmental capital has the feature of being *irreversible*" (the stratospheric ozone layer or a cool climate): once consumed, it can only be replaced with great difficulty if at all (Pearce 1989). Lost species cannot be recreated or the global climate cooled. Because we know little about the services natural ecosystems provide and how they operate, we should exercise caution in trading natural goods for "satanic mills" or education.

We know even less about the problem of " 'downstream' consequences of pollution" and the long-term effects of external inputs into homeostatic ecosystems (Rees 1990).

The division between ecological income and capital is also unclear. Is it conserving capital to log out all virgin forests and replace them with tree farms? Would not the resultant loss of biodiversity be a loss of natural capital? Is the construction of a space station and of a spaceship able to journey to Mars an appropriate increase in human and physical capital? As the rate at which sinks can process human wastes is generally unknown, their "income" cannot be calculated.

Ecological economics offers a corrective and a more appropriate, though only yet partial, narrative of an economy *for* sustaining development. Humans have non-economic roles that ecological economics recognizes, through inclusion of analytical approaches drawn from other social science disciplines. A policy approach constructed around this nascent economic model would greatly increase the importance of societal preferences and ecosystem needs, both of which imply significant social (government) intervention in the economy.

CONCLUSION

In adapting to uncertain ecological limits, an understanding of the economy in terms of a mechanical model that privileges market freedom misdirects policy. The market efficiently allocates scarce resources in the satisfaction of myriad diverse individual utility preferences. But the ungoverned market may encourage consumption, fails to appropriately price and trade natural resources, and does not protect sinks. Individual resource owners may not consume their natural assets at a rate that is socially or ecologically efficient.

In principle, government regulation of producer promotion and product prices is possible. However, other approaches would have less intrusive and probably more efficient influences on consumer choices, yet would avoid the draconian constraints of Daly's regulatory institutions. I shall suggest three policy approaches. First, products and services could be taxed based on their natural goods content. Second, consumption could be directly taxed. Third, marketable quotas and permits for natural goods usage could be assigned to producers.

As the objective of a Natural Goods Use Tax (NGU Tax) should be to satisfy the greatest quantity of human wants with the least amount of natural goods, rates of taxation would be in direct proportion to the quantity of natural goods consumed in the production of each good or service. Tax could be levied on the natural goods consumed in each stage of production comparably to modern value-added taxes. As there is no evidence that government revenues need to be significantly increased to sustain development, the NGU Tax could progressively replace taxation of labor, which is the mainstay of government revenue in modern economies.

An NGU Tax would also help to bring natural goods into the market. The market value of a natural good is now determined in the short term by its supply and demand and over the long term in relation to its cost of production. Ideally, the cost of a natural good used in production should also include a value representing the depletion of the stock or the productive capacity of a natural good. The technical problems in assessing that value are substantial, though various measures of contingent value represent a move in the right direction, especially with respect to sink consumption.

As discussed, the disparity of social and personal discount rates may be insoluble. A lower cost of money would increase the number of ecologically beneficial projects (with low rates of financial return) that individual resource owners could select from. However, interest rate manipulation is a primary means for governments to regulate the rate of economic activity, unemployment, and inflation. A lower rate of interest tends to encourage capital investment and consumption. For sustainable development, capital investment to increase eco-efficiency would be beneficial, consumption generally would not be. An NGU Tax should help to direct capital investment into eco-efficient options and to reduce consumption choices that demand greater quantities of natural goods. *Ceteris paribus*, lower discount rates aid sustainable development. However, subsidizing interest rates for selected eco-efficient investment would be more efficient though politically contentious.

If consumers use material goods to construct their identities, markets encourage consumption. The range of goods from competing producers advertising their products gives a myriad of opportunities to construct and reconstruct selves. Income and wealth disparities, which can be exacerbated by the market, will enhance the pressure of self-construction on consumption. Restricting consumption opportunities reduces consumer freedom, a core value of markets.[28] In recent political debate around tax reform in the United States, a consumption tax has been largely overlooked. A consumption tax would levy a tax on that part of income not saved and invested. With an appropriate personal or family allowance, it would avoid the problem of regression that purchase taxes—for example, sales and value-added taxes—impose. It also might reduce consumption and increase savings and investment, which could be directed to increasing production eco-efficiency. However, consumers still may demand goods and services that are eco-inefficient.

Evolutionary economics (discussed in more detail in the next chapter) focuses on how markets encourage adaptability in economic actors. This adaptability can be used to increase eco-efficiency more directly through natural goods use permits. This approach has been used to encourage innovation in the consumption of partially privatized natural goods. For example, in the United States, power generation plants are granted tradeable emissions permits, and in New Zealand fishermen are granted tradeable fish quotas. However, for sustainable development, such natural goods permit and quota plans should include a steadily decreasing total consumption of the specific natural goods. For example, the allowed total amount of emissions from power generation in the United States could be slowly reduced in a completely transparent policy process that mandates progressive emissions reductions by specified future dates. The power generation industry would be able to anticipate future emissions reductions and plan (and innovate) accordingly.

These suggestions are contentious, requiring a substantial shift in government preferences for market activities.[29] No taxation is socially neutral, and tax policies are often used for social engineering as much as raising revenue. Shifting from taxes on income, wealth, and capital to taxes on natural goods usage may be bitterly opposed by many industries including automobile, energy, paper, and construction. Individuals, groups, and sectors of the economy will win or lose.

Any discussion of such social engineering is premature. First a model of the market as a nonteleological life form rather than a machine must be broadly accepted. A machine can produce whatever humans design it to make; a life form is much less controllable. Markets do not have purposes of their own and market outcomes are rarely predictable. However, to ensure its own continued existence, this life form must adapt to the demands of its social and ecological environments. Acceptance of the economy as a complex adaptive system (which ecological economics approximates) will radically change the conventional wisdom about the innocence of markets that is reflected in the efficiency narrative and will result in policies that aid in adaptation to ecological limits.

# 4

## ORGANIZING A TECHNOLOGICAL FIX

Although direct methods for reducing fertility are often politically untenable, it is popular to contend that population growth is the principal cause of unsustainable development (for example, Ehrlich and Ehrlich 1974 and 1991; Ehrlich 1968; Hardin 1968). Such assertions assume that the "environmental footprint" of each human will remain the same or increase. In also distaining arguments that limits on want satisfaction will be necessary, the efficiency narrative expects that technological advances alone will reduce the impact of each human on ecological systems and can sufficiently reduce the overall human demand for natural goods.[1] The efficiency narrative simultaneously asserts that a capitalist free market system also is the best economic environment in which to produce the necessary technology: "Technology and the right political system—these are indeed the necessary and perhaps even the sufficient ingredients" for sustainable development (Singer 1992, 160).

Even some admitted technophobic advocates of sustainable development accept the benefits of free-market production of technology (Speth 1989). Technological innovations driven by the oil price increases of the 1970s reduced energy demand in the 1980s despite a growing world economy. Potential new technologies offer disease-resistant crops that require minimal fertilization, bioengineered animal protein, a paperless society, molecular design of products and customized microproduction, electricity from solar energy at nearly zero marginal cost, pollution-free hydrogen-powered cars, and everlasting and nonpolluting fusion reactors.[2] Technological innovation is likely to contribute enormously to the project of sustaining development.[3] But if technology alone is to sustain development—a specific objective—its production cannot be serendipitous; it must be chosen for its suitability to the task.

37

In the industrialized countries, governments have long aided and directed technological innovation, through military procurement or standard setting (Thurow 1986; Smith 1985); fiscal incentives (Mansfield 1982; Webre and Bodde 1986; Bozeman and Link 1984); environmental regulations (Brown et al. 1995); or grants and contracts with firms and universities (Rothwell and Dodgson 1992; Lederman 1994). While the greatest number of innovations have resulted from market-driven competition among profit-seeking firms, major innovations such as integrated circuits, supercomputers, and digital control of manufacturing have often been the direct result of government funded research (Noble 1984). Also, much basic scientific research that may eventually lead to important innovations is funded through political organizations. Despite the evident effectiveness of government funded research and development (R&D), people continue to debate about the extent to which governments should direct or participate in the process of technological innovation.[4] However, for the present purpose we can pose a different question: What is the best way to produce the technology needed to reduce the total human consumption of natural goods without artificially restraining human wants, while population continues to increase?

This chapter examines how the technological innovations appropriate to the goal of sustaining development can be selected in advance and effectively pursued. The first section considers the extent of the technological change required to sustain development: a shift to an ecological techno-economic paradigm. Next, the major theories on technological innovation are reviewed. This section concludes that present understanding of the process is inadequate for guiding necessary political intervention in the technological innovation process. The third section assesses the social factors that inhibit technological change and that may misdirect the innovation process. The fourth section considers the policies that might choose an ecological techno-economic paradigm and sustain development through technology. A concluding section reviews the problems with relying on technological innovation to sustain development.

## TECHNOLOGY AND INNOVATION

Technology may be broadly defined as "the application of scientific and other knowledge to practical tasks by ordered systems that involve people and organizations, living things and machines" (Pacey 1983, 6). It is a body of knowledge regarding the industrial arts together with the machines that embody such knowledge (Freeman 1977, 235).

Early research suggested that technological innovation was the result of scientific research, the mad inventor in a lonely laboratory or a scientist in a research institute (Bernal 1989; Rosenberg 1994). It was commonly believed that the search for new knowledge of natural processes created new materials and better methods for solving social problems (Bush 1946).[5] Science pushed through new scientific knowledge into new technology. This belief—reflected in government funding for university research and its own laboratories—reached its zenith immediately after World War II (Bernal 1989; Rosenberg 1994). Later research showed that some innovation was almost entirely the result of market demand: what has been called market or demand "pull" (Schmookler 1966; Mowery and Rosenberg 1979). The current consensus view is that technological innovation is "a coupling process, which first takes place in the minds of imaginative people somewhere at the ever changing interface between science, technology and the market" (Freeman 1979). In market economies this process occurs primarily within profit-seeking firms that create new products or design a more efficient production system or a new way of ordering and connecting technical operations.[6] Both science-push and demand-pull usually play a part in technological innovation, but their relative importance varies between industries, within industries over time, and with size of firm (Sahal 1981; Freeman 1992, 73–120; Mowery and Rosenberg 1979; Walsh 1984).

Technological innovations may be categorized as incremental or radical, or as changes in technology systems or techno-economic paradigm (Freeman 1992, 194–199). It is probable that a sustainably developing human society would be founded upon an "ecological" techno-economic paradigm in which technologies are selected primarily for their eco-efficiency.

*Incremental innovations* are small changes in widely available technologies. These include firm-specific modifications to production technologies and the continual marginal improvements in the efficiency of the internal combustion engine, many in response to government regulation.[7] Even mature technologies can be improved in a series of small incremental steps; these are often proprietary changes to process technologies that are never patented and may not be marketed. Incremental innovations, from learning by doing and learning by using, are firm responses to market pressures to reduce process costs or improve product quality.[8]

*Radical innovations* are discontinuous changes in production systems, usually resulting from new scientific knowledge. When synthetic fibers such as nylon and polyester replaced cotton and other natural clothing fibers in many plants, their different handling requirements and capabilities demanded redesigned production systems. Such innovations represent a nonlinear change from prior products or processes; incrementally improving natural fibers will never produce nylon and, as Schumpeter argued, no increase in the number of mail coaches will construct a railway (quoted in Freeman 1992, 79). Radical innovations spawn new markets and subsequent incremental innovations.

*Technology systems* are clusters of related radical innovations. Examples include steam ships, railways, commercial airliners, and semiconductors. They create new industries and new markets, radically changing or more often replacing old industries and spinning off other new industries. By the 1950s, when commercial airliners had developed sufficiently to regularly and safely cross the Atlantic, the life of the oceangoing liner (dominant in the 1930s) was at an end. Semiconductors have created the brave new world of microcomputers, automated coffeepots, climate control systems, compact disk players, and fuel-efficient automobile engines.

*A new techno-economic paradigm* is a rare event that revolutionizes the technological and economic logic used to satisfy human wants. New paradigms are " 'creative gales of destruction' or successive industrial revolutions which are at the heart of Schumpeter's long wave theory. They represent those new technology systems which have such pervasive effects on the economy as a whole that they change the style of production and management throughout the economy. The introduction of electric power or steam power are examples of such profound transformations. . . . The electronic computer and microelectronics are at the heart of such a paradigm today" (Freeman 1992, 196). First came the "natural" paradigm, then steam power, electric power, and mass production.[9] Finally, the present (fifth) information and communication technology paradigm. Just as the introduction of electric power changed the products and processes of all industries, so has information technology become embedded throughout the economy and society. Development could be sustained by technology alone if the next techno-economic paradigm is ecological. The probability would be enhanced that this paradigm shift could sustain development indefinitely if it occurred sooner rather than later.

Techno-economic paradigms evolve from marrying a myriad of technological advances in a wide range of products and processes. The most recent paradigm resulted from an accumulation of innovations in diverse sectors—materials, electronics, production engineering, computing and software design theory, telephony, and organizational design. An ecological techno-economic paradigm would incorporate technologies that individually and together minimize natural goods consumption without constraining development choices. It would require new materials, production systems, and organizational arrangements, even new technology systems, and would be the result of the conscious pursuit of all possible technological means to minimize natural goods consumption. The rest of this chapter considers how an ecological techno-economic paradigm may be selected to sustain development.

Because technological innovation is closely connected to the production system, economic analysis has increasingly become the predominant means for theorizing about the factors in macro-level innovation.[10] The two principal approaches are neoclassical and evolutionary economics, both of which reflect a market-pull orientation and treat basic scientific research as exogenous.

*Neoclassical* economic theories of economic growth emphasize the role of capital accumulation in increasing the efficiency of resource use. When high levels of capital have been accumulated, technological innovation for cost reduction becomes an important component in profit maximization by firms in the market (Salter 1960; David 1975; Mansfield 1968).

Technology is assumed to be freely available and known to all firms in the perfectly competitive market. Although in practice production techniques are discontinuous and discrete, neoclassical theory assumes that there is a continuous range of technologies that mix capital and labor in different ratios for a single desired output level. Changes in the relative cost of factors of production are a major spur to innovation and "to invention of a particular kind—directed to economizing the use of a factor which has become relatively more expensive" (Hicks, quoted in Elster 1983, 101). However, if all firms adopt the same technology to reduce their consumption of labor, the prevailing wage rate will fall and the early adopter's advantage will be extinguished. Aside from this generalized expectation, neoclassical theory focuses on the quantity of innovation as a means to increase profits and further investment, without considering other purposes for innovation.

If the assumption of cost-free access to technology is removed, neoclassical theory recognizes the structure of demand and the stock of capital as important causes of innovation (David 1975; Salter 1960). In addition to reducing the consumption of the relatively costly factor of production, firms may seek to adjust to shifts in demand or to modify process efficiency through investment in research and development. Neoclassical theory can explain local incremental innovations that result from learning by doing and learning by using (Dosi 1982; David 1975; Arrow 1962; Sahal 1981:202) but is ineffective at explaining more radical innovation. Given the rarity and complexity of novel techno-economic paradigms, it is unlikely that the mechanistic neoclassical theory could explain their occurrence.

*Evolutionary theory* derives from the work of Joseph Schumpeter, who separated the concepts of invention from innovation and diffusion of technology and focused attention on the occasional radical innovations produced by entrepreneurs who accept huge risks because they operate on will rather than intellect. In arguing for a less mechanistic explanation of economic growth, he promoted the importance of the small innovative firm that can drive out large entrenched businesses in a "gale of creative destruction" (Schumpeter 1934).[11] Evolutionary theories built on Schumpeter's concepts deliberately mimic models of biological processes but do not exactly replicate them.

The competitive market "selects" certain capabilities of firms: "the core concern of evolutionary theory is with the dynamic process by which firm behavior patterns and market outcomes are jointly determined over time" (Nelson and Winter 1982, 18).[12] Those firms that are most effective at designing and adopting successful behaviors increase their market power. Firms' adaptive behaviors in response to the selection mechanism of the market are conscious and teleological rather than random genetic modifications. Such behaviors may include research and development activities and innovative process and product modifications.

Evolutionary economics explains incremental and radical innovations and offers a more complete and accurate description of the relationship between firms' R&D and marketing efforts and more basic scientific research. For example, Nelson (1995) comments that scientists employed in industrial laboratories are often encouraged to publish their research in order to establish the scientific credentials of the laboratory and thus to attract other good research scientists. However, while this approach explains the level of innovative activity, it cannot predict the quality or type of technological innovation beyond satisfaction of firms' goals of continued existence and increased profits. Nor can it explain how ecologically efficient technological innovations will be produced if they are not demanded in the market.

The dominance in evolutionary economics of a demand-based selection mechanism reflects the greater numerical importance of incremental and radical innovations, which occur many orders of magnitude more frequently than techno-economic paradigm shifts. Because evolutionary economic theory measures the quantity rather than the quality of scientific effort, except in so far as quality is measured by market demand satisfied, it fits well with reality. Thus, evolutionary theory suggests how governments may vary the quantity of innovation—such as by encouraging competition, reducing the net costs to firms' of their search for effective behaviors (R&D and organization changes), increasing the return to innovation (as through patent and copyright protection), and increasing the rate of transfer of technical knowledge between scientific enterprise (as in universities) and firms (Nelson 1990; Lederman 1994; Dosi 1982; Clark 1990; Mansfield 1968). But by according governments a peripheral role in technological innovation, it suggests no way for society collectively to choose a qualitative change in technology except through uncoordinated activities in the market.

A shift to a new techno-economic paradigm is the outcome of a large number of apparently random changes in scientific knowledge that are not recognized as connected at the time they occur. For the paradigm shift to be designed rather than serendipitous, it must be possible to anticipate the components of the new paradigm and to direct the system of technological innovation toward those paradigm components; and social institutions must not inhibit the change. The next section reviews the structural factors that inhibit technological change and may prevent a paradigm shift.

## STRUCTURAL INHIBITORS

Social inertia, scientific and engineering professionalism, and uncertainty about the future uses of scientific knowledge may divert technology from any planned development. Even if governments took responsibility for stimulating the innovations believed necessary to sustain development, they would be unable to achieve their purpose.

### Social Inertia

Many knowledgeable people who are not Luddites can fear the social consequences of rapid technological change. Advancing technology could lead to more leisure; it is capitalism that interprets more leisure as unemployment for some and a full workday for others. Even if technology does not replace human labor, it inevitably changes lifestyles, work demands, and social relations.[13] The social effects of new technologies are almost impossible to estimate (Rosenberg 1994; Rosenberg and Birdzell 1990) and, while society adapts to technology, it may do so reluctantly and in unpredictable ways.[14] The habits of humanity, investment in the sunk cost of old technologies, and slow social learning have always made prediction of future technologies a precarious business (Rosenberg 1995). Commuter frustration derives from a habitual workday structure (eight to five) but the spread of telecommuting is inhibited by a human need for social contact in the workplace. The design of modern cities with extensive suburbs and distributed industry, together with the trillions of dollars of investment in gasoline-powered automobiles and their supporting industries discourage, through consumer choice and the political influence of interested firms, conversion to mass transit or to zero-emission vehicles. Institutionalization of historical work practices does nothing to encourage workers to accept new technologies or change their personal habits.

## Protective Professionalism

Basic science research seeks to understand the world better; it is not directed by the usefulness of the knowledge it produces. The quality of method, both theoretical and empirical, is a primary measure of the quality of the scientific product: a good scientist is one who does good science. Scientists and engineers have disaggregated into autonomous "invisible colleges" that have a "guild-like communality" of the tools and instrumentalities of their work (Price 1983).

Because of the communality of science and the need for peer review and evaluation,[15] the process of science is one of small accretions to a core body of knowledge, rather as a crystal grows. It is "a series of step-by-step advances in a tradition which Thomas Kuhn calls 'normal science' " (Price 1983). From "a central core laid down at the beginning in the mid-seventeenth century invention of the scientific paper . . . each annual co-citation map is laid down like successive skins of an irregular onion." Action tends to develop where there has been earlier action; "a piece can only be fitted to the puzzle if the puzzle has grown to exactly that stage that will accommodate the new piece at its research front border." New instrumentation, growth in related areas of science, or the application of a new empirical method attract research funding and researchers to a specific area of science. The desire for their colleagues' approbation also encourages scientists to pursue "hot" research within their specialties. Although some scientists, such as members of the Union of Concerned Scientists, are driven by their personal values to pursue environmentally benign research or to oppose socially and environmentally destructive research, the great majority of scientific researchers pursue their specialty with little or no concern for its potential environmental risks. In their defense, it may not be possible to identify the environmental risks of each research project, just as (I argue below) it is frequently not possible to identify the basic research that will be environmentally beneficial. The microprocessor was not designed to enhance energy efficiency, but that is its role in many production control systems.

Engineering is a pragmatic and practical discipline, yet it, too, has an internal dynamic—"professional standards"—that often makes engineers ignore many of the environmental impacts of their work. Trained to use a rational, scientific method to find solutions to practical problems, engineers measure the quality of their solutions by the standards of the profession. Social and economic concerns may be of less importance than the engineering "sweetness" of the solution (Wells 1984), and environmental impacts are often even less of a measure of engineering quality. The small amount of discussion of ethics in the engineering profession rarely extends to consideration of the ecological consequences of engineering design. As in business ethics, the concern is primarily for honest, plain dealing with clients and employees and delivery of "quality" work (Schlossberger 1993; Cottell 1993). Few engineering scholars show a rudimentary concern for ecological issues (Gunn and Vesilind 1986). Unusually, Coates (1993) calls for the integration of engineering with other disciplines within projects to ensure that the "fairly narrow view" of most engineers is expanded.

The internal dynamics of the scientific and engineering professions are significant factors in the direction and rate of change of technology. The training and methods of scientists and engineers intended to maintain professional standards may be antithetical to human and ecological systems maintenance over the very long term.

## Prediction Problems

Forecasting is a linear science; it assumes that the future will echo history. Thus, it also assumes a certain regularity in human systems. Yet, there is some evidence that the expected relatively predictable flow of incrementally enhanced technologies can become disrupted, and the naturally selected, most "fit" technology may not lead to selection of the "best" technology: "with the acceptance of positive feedbacks, economists' theories are beginning to portray the economy not as simple but as complex, not as deterministic, predictable and mechanistic but as process-dependent, organic and always evolving" (Arthur 1990). Examples of suboptimal technologies include the QWERTY keyboard, VHS video recording, and the Intel 8088 microprocessor (Arthur 1990; David 1985). Early computer models of complexity built upon biological processes are surprisingly successful at representing economic activity (Waldrop 1992; Arthur 1989, 1988).

While economists usually assume that technological innovations develop smoothly in response to prices and demand, "positive-feedback" economics suggests that technologies may " 'phase lock' into one of many possible configurations; small perturbations at critical times influence which outcome is selected, and the chosen outcome may have higher energy (that is, be less favorable) than other possible states" (Arthur

1990). From the infinite range of technological futures, one is selected for any of a myriad of reasons that may have little to do with either economic interests or ecological necessity. Thus, technologies that are more than incrementally innovative are largely indeterminate.

These new theories of positive feedback in the economy suggest that market-driven technological choices may be technically suboptimal, offering a bleaker prospect for a techno-economic paradigm shift. They also model the economy as blindly evolving in response to a set of rules that, while simple, do not permit prediction of the development path. Small perturbations early in the process of technological development or within the selection mechanism may have very large effects in the future; small suboptimal technological choices may *prevent* a shift to a more ecological techno-economic paradigm.

## CHOOSING AN ECOLOGICAL TECHNO-ECONOMIC PARADIGM

Because techno-economic paradigm shifts are such rare and complex phenomena, theories of technological innovation are not designed to explain their causes, to predict when they will occur, nor to explain how to bring them about. Knowing what generates a large number of incremental innovations does not indicate what factors will produce a shift to a new techno-economic paradigm. Incremental innovations are direct responses to market demand, to marginally increase product quality or function or to reduce product cost. What has not been invented cannot be demanded, except abstractly.[16] But as innovations become more radical, science-push becomes more important. This implies that planning of investment in basic and applied scientific research to choose a path to an ecological techno-economic paradigm will be important.

Although current theories suggest policies to adjust the quantity of innovation, they do not explain how to create a specific set of technological innovations that would lead onto and along a path of sustainable development. Economic research into technological innovation treats all innovations as equivalent events; little effort is made to discern those innovations that will have a greater impact on society or will contribute more to a techno-economic paradigm shift.[17]

If the economy is a complex adaptive system, neither can specific technologies be predicted nor can a process be designed to ensure that they can be produced. It is also generally assumed that the requisite ecologically friendly technologies can be "discovered"—as if they lie in wait for the scientific searcher who seeks them in the right place. This belief underlies economic approaches that measure research effort and quantity of technology produced; but it is possible that some imagined future ecological technologies might not be possible.

The conclusions of this chapter have implications both for theory and practical policy. A primary purpose of theory is to guide practice. If technology is to sustain development, theory must include advances in scientific knowledge as an endogenous variable to better explain how science constrains and directs technology. Policy should recognize that to increase production of ecologically friendly technologies and create a shift to an ecological techno-economic paradigm will require (1) modifying the market selection mechanism to change consumer preferences and, thus, their market behaviors; (2) providing incentives to firms to choose technological and administrative innovations for their ecological benefits; (3) intervening to prevent social resistance to the necessary changes in technology; and (4) increasing government support for basic scientific research and a change in the organization of the selection of projects for funding.

## Theory Implications

There is not the space to elaborate a significant modification to evolutionary economics. However, in order to explain a techno-economic paradigm shift, this theory must reflect the selection mechanism of technical sweetness and advance in scientific knowledge. Modeling the technology process as a complex adaptive system incorporating behavioral rules for scientists, engineers, firms, consumers, and governments would reflect the true indeterminacy of the real innovation process. A model that reasonably accurately reconstructed prior paradigm shifts might indicate the probability of achieving sustainable development through technology and where exogenous stimulation in the process would be most effective. Despite the absence of such a model, we can identify some directions for technology policy. First, market selection of technology could be influenced through consumer demand. Second, firms' incentives could be modified by publishing measures of their eco-efficiency. Third, the education and reward systems for scientists and engineers could specifically include consideration of the ecological impacts of their choices. Fourth, government funding of basic research could be increased and a greater number of smaller bets made on a wider range of potential technologies.

## Changing Consumer Preferences

As a positive theory of market-based activities, evolutionary economics assumes *homo economicus*, the rational, self-interested economic actor who assesses the utility of alternative behaviors in terms of her material wants and economic capabilities. The environmental selection mechanism is the sum of the demands of such consumers coupled with the desire of producers to optimize their market power and profits; in the market, everyone is paid according to his contribution to the satisfaction of others' wants. If consumer wants satisfied in the market were constituted less of material desires and more of nonmaterial desires, including aesthetic valuation of eco-systems, firms would be rewarded through the market for reducing their consumption of natural goods.[18] This might be achieved by educating consumers on the ecological impacts of their consumption choices and might include education in the ethical regard for nonhuman life, often considered to be the critical missing piece in "greening" society (see chapter 7). Both governments and nongovernmental organizations may play a part in the green education of consumers, and both are involved now in most industrialized countries in such a task. Despite the assertions of some business groups (e.g., see Schmidheiny 1992), there is no guarantee that the right kind of green innovations will be selected by consumers.

## Ecological Selection

Firms' behavior could be more directly influenced by measuring and rewarding firm performance in reducing natural goods consumption. Just as audited financial statements are the basis of an equity market valuation of firm performance, publication of a firm's ecological efficiency using standard measures (as accepted by the Security and Exchange Commission or its equivalent) may directly (through capital markets) and indirectly (through public and consumer opinion) pressure firms to choose eco-efficient technologies. Similar effects may result from differentially taxing ecologically inefficient activities, as chapter 3 proposes. Markets in tradeable pollution permits (as in the United States for SOx) are an adaptation of this approach (Repetto 1992).

## Overcoming Social Inertia

It is not readily apparent how governmental intervention might reduce the inhibitory effects of social structures and habits. However, government could directly influence scientists' and engineers' inclusion of ecological ethics in their professional decisions. Funding of basic research could prioritize ecological research—as in the Cold War, defense-related research dominated scientific decision making. Governments might also indirectly influence perceptions of professionalism by sponsoring open discourse on the issue among scientists and engineers. Governments are less effective at predicting which scientific and technological developments will be profitable than profit-motivated firms (Hill and

Utterback 1979). It is no more likely that governments would be any better able to predict which technologies were important for the new ecological techno-economic paradigm and then to ensure their efficient pursuit.

## Funding Basic Research

It is not possible to identify in advance all the scientific and technological developments that will be necessary to sustain development. While an ecological techno-economic paradigm may result from random incremental or radical innovations resulting from the self-interested utility maximization in a competitive market, the central problem is social choice of technology for its expected ecological benefit. It is counterintuitive that the necessary components of a techno-economic paradigm can be known in advance. Shockley invented the transistor in response to a localized problem of the high cost and poor reliability of computer components, not anticipating the future market demand for pocket radios, personal computers, and fax machines. When IBM had produced its first prototype computer, its chief executive predicted a global market of a few hundred units for the product. Bell Laboratories initially refused to patent the laser, unable to foresee commercial applications (Rosenberg 1995).

Because firms adapt available scientific knowledge much more than they create it themselves, and because the social benefits of innovation exceed the private benefits (and this is even more the case in the search for sustainable development through an ecological techno-economic paradigm), a shotgun approach to R&D investment—especially in basic and applied scientific research funded through political institutions—would be more effective than attempting to hit technological targets that are predicted to increase eco-efficiency. As the knowledge necessary for an ecological techno-economic paradigm cannot be predicted, government funding of basic research should be increased in its total amount and in the number of projects funded.

Gore (1992) has suggested a Marshall Plan for Planet Earth. A more appropriate model for government intervention might be the U.S. Department of Defense direction (through the Defense Advanced Research Products Agency, DARPA) of basic research for military technologies. Through standard setting and funding of exploratory basic research DARPA stimulated design of critical consumer and production technologies such as the microprocessor and digitally controlled production systems (Wilson et al. 1980; Noble 1984; Smith 1985). Investment in basic and applied research with the objective of an ecological techno-economic paradigm would not necessarily reduce economic growth.[19] Countries that institute a national objective of ecological technology will probably reap trade gains while helping to sustain development globally and reducing their dependence on natural goods.

CONCLUSION

Neither jointly nor severally will these suggested government policies ensure that technological innovations will sustain development. Society needs to adapt to the demands of ecological limits as well as to the technologies developed to reduce natural goods consumption directly. Human ecology offers a model of society as an adaptive mechanism, based in the connections between individuals (see Hawley 1986). More explicit connection between human ecology theories (based in sociology) and evolutionary economics should enhance understanding of technological innovation as one aspect of a complete social adaptive response.

This chapter has demonstrated first that reliance on technological innovation to sustain development is neither a panacea nor a socially cost-free movement in the right direction. Second, it has argued that collectives must, through political institutions, consciously choose the knowledge and technologies that will lead to an ecological techno-economic paradigm. Sustainable development cannot be assured through the mechanism of private innovation in a market economy. Rather as five thousand monkeys may eventually type *Hamlet*, the market with a demand selection mechanism may hit on the necessary technologies. The probability of producing the eco-efficient technologies required to move to an ecological techno-economic paradigm would be greatly enhanced with some judicious intervention in the free market by political institutions.

The preceding chapter also concluded that, in the efficiency narrative, use of the language, concepts, and methods of neoclassical economics had lead it to define the problem of sustainable development incorrectly and to offer incomplete or incorrect policy solutions. The efficiency narrative assigns too small a role to political institutions and organizations in sustainable development. The next two chapters consider the equity narrative, which assigns a central role to politics in sustainable development.

# 5

## CONSIDERING EQUITY

An economist has commented: "If you said, 'Let's design a problem that human institutions can't deal with,' you couldn't find one better than global warming" (Jacoby, quoted in Lemonick 1995). You can though: sustainable development. In the equity narrative, sustainable development is understood as the problem of the just distribution of natural limits, or of their insufficiency, in order to reduce the impact of those limits on communities and, thus, individuals. It is the problem of distributing a limited supply of natural goods between individuals, between countries, and between generations. This is inherently a problem of politics.

Politics has been variously defined as the authoritative allocation of valued things; who gets what, when, and how; and an us versus them clash of interest groups. A classical definition is "the deliberate and self-conscious creation of the structures and norms governing our collective lives, where the focus is on the political as at least potentially a sphere of human freedom."[1] For the present purpose, politics may be defined positively as the means by which collectives (nations, states, societies, cities, and other communities of all types and sizes) distribute the benefits of collective life. Normatively it can be understood as the arena for optimizing individual human freedom through collective life. For every member of a collective to benefit from that membership requires that the benefits of collective life are distributed equitably, although it is impossible to define equity objectively.[2]

Hitherto I have referred to "government" on a number of occasions. Chapter 3 concluded that some government intervention in the market will be necessary to sustain development; chapter 4 concluded with suggestions for government intervention in the process of technological innovation to create an ecological techno-economic paradigm. By government, I mean that collection of institutions by which a collective governs its public space and solves communal problems. The design and operation of the institutions of governance are the stuff of politics and the heart of the equity narrative. If, as this narrative argues, sustainable development is a collective problem requiring coordinated action, only the just collectives will be able to encourage the individual behaviors and to organize the social interactions that will sustain development. In such collectives, individuals act for the common good because they perceive that their society is fair, that the process and result of politics is equitable.[3]

This chapter investigates the tension between individual liberty and effective communal action. The first section examines the need for authority in creating an effective collective response to the problem of ecological limits. This section explicitly considers the political implications of steady-state economics discussed in chapter 3. The next section seeks an understanding of the conflict between individual liberty and communal cohesion in political theory. The third section summarizes and critiques rational choice, the dominant approach in political science. This methodology cannot explain and may actually inhibit the political processes necessary for sustainable development. The fourth section outlines a model of politics that should balance individual and collective interests and might effectively sustain development. A short conclusion outlines the lessons to be learned from the equity narrative's strengths and weaknesses.

## THE NEED FOR AUTHORITY

The range and complexity of problems that ecological limits present to human society suggests to many theorists a necessary dominance of the needs of the collective over the individual. A technocratic state or a technocratic/environmentalist elite—perhaps like Plato's philosopher kings (Ophuls and Boyan 1992)—is proposed as part of the solution to environmental crisis by a number of authors (including Ophuls and Boyan 1992 and Milbrath 1984) to make the tough and technically complicated decisions of which democracy is incapable.[4] Experts could make "scientific" or "rational" decisions based on the best available knowledge for the benefit of the community as a whole, bypassing special interest groups (Schmandt 1981). Other analysts, while not advocating technocracy, are concerned about the failure of large groups of self-seeking individuals to provide public goods (Olson 1965) and are skeptical of the benefits of democracy (Ferry 1995).[5] If these "ecological mandarins" have no hard knowledge of human cause and natural effect (or consequent human effect) they are little better able to make effective policy choices than more democratic forms of governance. Analytical approaches that assume—as does ecological economics—that the economy is embedded in the social and political community and the natural environment also tend to favor the collective over the individual. Herman Daly's steady-state economics neatly illustrates this problem.

Daly has long advocated a steady-state economy as the best way for an industrialized country to sustain development. To achieve a steady-state economy requires social (or political) institutions to ensure sufficient distributional equality, to cap population growth, and to limit the rate of consumption of natural resources, all for the purpose of limiting the economic throughput. Of Daly's three institutions, the "critical" one is the distribution institution: "exchange relations are mutually beneficial among relative equals" (Daly 1991, 54–55). But present wealth and income inequalities make the market, that is itself morally neutral, an unjust social institution. He proposes a maximum limit on incomes and wealth through a progressive income tax up to a marginal 100 percent rate and an adequate minimum wage that would allow the outlawing of strikes. Limits could be adjusted if the difference between upper and lower incomes and wealth limits became a disincentive to effort. Additional regulation of the size of corporations and their ability to accumulate capital would be necessary (Daly 1991, 56).

Population growth would be restricted by granting to each woman limited and transferable birth licenses. Because licenses could be traded, the rich might bear more children than the poor but the market in licenses would tend to equalize wealth in the process. The rich would benefit, but as Daly notes, they always do. State regulation of childbearing is practiced in China, and Daly argues that it is not an unreasonable restraint of liberty to ensure sustainable development.

An institution would also regulate extraction of natural resources through depletion quotas. These would restrict the annual depletion of natural resources reserves even on private land to an amount considered appropriate. Innovation in production technology would be required to maintain consumer want satisfaction within a quota-induced shortage of inputs.

Each of these institutions reflects a priority of collective over individual rights (a dictatorship of the many over the one?) permitting or even requiring an authoritarian government. Perhaps Daly, as an economist, is appropriately less concerned with how these institutions would be established and operated than with the needs of the economy. But this does illustrate the difficulty of balancing technical economic solutions with the essential human freedoms that comprise much of development.

Maintaining a certain material affluence in a steady-state and ecologically sustainable economy at the expense of individual human rights and essential political freedoms is not sustainable development. What is required is governance that optimizes the benefits of collective life, permitting effective communal action to avoid exceeding ecological limits, while simultaneously enhancing individual liberty. This is the concern of political theory. The next section reviews the continuing debate within political theory on how to balance individual freedoms with a robust community from which all individuals may draw a just benefit.

Contemporary versions of liberalism underpin the modern mixed economy welfare state; these were generally accepted throughout the industrialized countries for the majority of the twentieth century. Even the international system can be said to have liberalism "embedded" within it (Ruggie 1983, 198–199). Liberalism is primarily concerned with safeguarding the rights of the individual, communitarianism with the rights of the community, which potentially conflict with the rights of individuals. Because liberalism and Marxism are more similar than usually believed (see Kymlicka 1989, 1990; Morrice 1994; and Gilbert 1990), the discussion here is between a focus on the individual typified by contemporary liberal political theory and a community focus represented by communitarian political theory.[6] Communitarian political theories oppose what is seen as the communally destructive individuality of liberalism and argue for greater rights for the community.

## Individual Needs

Although both approaches treat individuals as ends in themselves, liberalism should not be confused with libertarianism. Libertarianism emphasizes the right to "self-ownership" and extends that right to ownership of property: "what owns and what is owned are one and the same, namely the whole person" (Cohen, quoted in Kymlicka 1990, 105). Locke's conception of property, which underlies libertarian thought, includes our life, liberty, and property (Locke 1980, 123–127); the modern conception, after Adam Smith's *Wealth of Nations*, is primarily limited to the latter term in the sense of material possessions. Thus, libertarian political theory is now an argument for property rights rather than positive liberty.

Libertarianism offers no moral basis for this primacy of property rights (Kymlicka 1990, 95–159). If property has been justly conveyed through time to the present and market outcomes are assumed to reflect the capacities of individuals, the present distribution is just if the initial distribution was just (Nozick 1974). The initial distribution is just if it is consistent with treating all members of society as equals; that is, if none is worse off as a result of the initial unequal accumulation of common property through enclosure of the commons. If the ownership of property increases liberty, then the non-ownership that ownership creates, reduces liberty. Only if there are unlimited quantities of equivalent property does my ownership not diminish your enjoyment of property. Unlike seventeenth century America, this is no longer the case. Under conditions of scarcity, property rights do not increase total liberty. Locke assumed that the market would compensate fairly through wages those who failed to gain property rights in the initial distribution; but this ownership of property assigns disproportionate market power, creating unjust compensation for non-property owners.[7]

In contrast, contemporary liberalism offers a broader, more positive conception of liberty: the freedom and ability to determine oneself. Classical liberalism was concerned with enhancing individual liberty and opposing the constraints on personal liberty imposed by utilitarianism's "greatest good of the greatest number." Contemporary liberalism starts from an assumption that the purpose of the political collective is to enhance the individual's ability to choose how to develop his or her capacities: "The attractive idea at the base of the prevailing view is that people's fate should be determined by their choices—by the decision they make about how to lead their lives—not by the circumstances in which they happen to find themselves" (Kymlicka 1990, 57, 75). Equity is then a matter of regulating "inequalities that affect people's life-chances, not the inequalities that arise from peoples's life-choices, which are the individual's own responsibility."[8]

Governments should play an active role through intervention in the market and redistributive mechanisms to ameliorate the accidental inequalities that influence life chances (Kymlicka 1989, 11–13; Hodgson 1994). Private ownership and market activity are acceptable, but "all social primary goods—liberty and opportunity, income and wealth, and the bases of self-respect—are to be distributed equally unless an unequal distribution of any or all of these goods is to the advantage of the least favored" (Rawls 1971, 303). While this distributional rule is not accepted by all liberals (and by few philosophers of other persuasions), it is a useful general guide to the nature of distributional rules in contemporary liberalism. Inequalities that benefit all—"by drawing out socially useful talents and energies"—may remain (Kymlicka 1990, 52).[9]

Because unrestrained self-interest through the market, as assumed in economics, would destroy social ties and beneficial cultural practices, individual liberty also must be restrained by concern for the condition of others and our effects upon their condition. Locke argued that acquisition of property (initially the product of land and then land itself) is justified by the application of labor, if "as much and as good" remains for everyone else and each takes no more than he or she needs (Schwarzenbach 1988). But Locke (1980, §37–40) recognized that the institution of the market released property owners from this ethical self-restraint. Although in the seventeenth century undeveloped land was still available, he did not advocate unlimited personal acquisition of property and in the case of the Virginia colony proposed regulations to prevent this from occurring (Kammen 1966). The idea of self-restraint in the pursuit of individual liberty was echoed late in the nineteenth century by John Stuart Mill (1974 [1859] ). Even the conservative Edmund Burke believed that "our passions forge our fetters" and that unrestrained pursuit of individual liberty invites state intervention to protect the commonwealth (cited Reynolds 1985, 197).

Some scholars conceive of self-restraint as mere toleration of others' ideas and interests in the pursuit of self-interest. Self-interest is not selfishness, acting without concern for the possible harm or neglect of others.[10] Self-restraint is a duty to actively consider the ideas and interests of others when acting (d'Entrèves 1990; Smith 1976), to have "sympathy" for others, an essential aspect of human behavior in communities, that is "essentially feeling *with* someone" (Campbell 1971, 94). This "organic connection" between members of a community overrides narrow self-interest so that "we should view ourselves, not in the light in which our own selfish passions are apt to place us, but in the light which any other citizen of the world would view us" (Smith 1976, 7, 140–141). Rawls, for example, argues that individuals have duties to others: a duty of mutual aid, duties not to harm others nor to cause unnecessary suffering, and a duty of justice (equity) that binds individuals generally to political institutions (Rawls 1971, 114–117, 333–355).

## Community Needs

Different strands of communitarian theory are united by the common belief that, because the community has rights, the ties that make community are important and should be defended. This criticism of the dominant individualist political theories has focused on the breakdown in "civicness," and the inevitable destruction of social cohesion and the natural environment by the libertarian capitalist market economy (Ophuls and Boyan 1992; "The Politics of Restoration"; Putnam 1993; O'Connor 1994).

A community is a group of individuals bound together by a "web of moral understandings and commitments" (Bellah et al. 1985,

335). Communitarians argue that communities also have rights and that individuals are not autonomous but are socially constructed. Not only do they constitute society, they are constituted by it: "individuality, so far from being the focal point of political values is only intelligible within the framework of an established community, which cannot be the product of choice" (Barry 1989, 28). The community gives our lives value and meaning and largely directs them.

Liberalism's promise was to free conceptions of rationality, equity, and justice from religious and cultural traditions. MacIntyre (1988) has argued that not only is this an unfulfilled promise but that it cannot be fulfilled; individuals are never able to separate themselves from their culture and traditions. The French, English, Scots, and Spaniards would more readily recognize this truth than would Americans; the sense of who you are is more definable in those countries and nationalities with long recognizable and distinct traditions. Individuals are not merely cognizant of others and concerned for their liberty, they are constructed by them, they are a part of the whole that cannot be separated from the traditions and cultures that distinguish the community (MacIntyre 1988, 326–348; Barry 1989, 115–118).

Individuals are not distinct from community, for moral action can only occur "within local forms of community united around a shared conception of the good" (d'Entrèves 1990, 79). Socially constituted individuals know 'the good' as members of the community, and cannot perceive it independently of community. Because the community constitutes the self, the good can only be pursued by the individual once first defined by the community through its ends and values. Thus, individual choice of good is largely fore-ordained by construction of the individual by the community, and equity "starts from a social conception of the individual and from acknowledgement of the primacy of the community" (81).

Communitarianism is the political theory of the common good. If the self is embedded in society, identity comes from society. Whereas in liberalism the state encourages a deeper immersion in oneself, the communitarian state respects that socially constrained self-determination by encouraging deeper immersion in the community. The communitarian state determines what is valuable and therefore the life projects from which individuals may select. In contrast, the liberal state seeks primarily to provide individuals with the liberty and resources to determine themselves through projects *they* decide are valuable; all human associations are voluntary, and government will only interfere in the activities of individuals to prevent "conduct deemed harmful or injurious in its consequences" (Lowi, quoted in Stever 1995, 487). Thus, the disagreement between liberals and communitarians is "not over the individual's dependence on society, but over society's dependence on the individual" (Kymlicka 1990, 208, 230).

## Balancing Needs

There is substantial disagreement about the meaning of development. However, development includes maintenance and enhancement of the ability of individuals to pursue their own projects as well as improvement of the conditions of communal life. As Goulet (1977, x) has commented, development is "a complex series of interrelated change processes, abrupt and gradual, by which a population and all its components move away from patterns of life perceived in some significant way as 'less human' toward alternative patterns of life perceived as 'more human.' . . . In the process new solidarities, extending to the entire world, must be created and cultural and ecological diversity must be nurtured. Finally, esteem and freedom for all individuals and societies must be optimized." Thus, sustainable development requires a solution to the problem long the bane of political theorists of balancing individual agency and community need.

In communitarian society, the individual is subordinate to the community and its purposes. Justice or equity is defined by communal tradition and not independently of community (MacIntyre 1988). Yet, rather than pursuing a single form of equity, the community could apply different forms of distributive justice appropriate to different situations, permitting a pragmatic, pluralistic interpretation of equity. This is not the pluralism of liberal theory, a pluralism of individual ideas and values for each situation and type of problem. Whereas liberal theory would encourage individuals to pursue their individual projects of self-determination in a world of ecological scarcity, in the communitarian society the community would provide guidance on equity and justice under conditions of ecological constraint. If the community's rights trump those of the individual, either traditions or moral codes will have conditioned individuals to accept a certain solution, or the government as the agent of the community will enforce a single conception of equity, a single set of values.

"Hard" communitarian theories, which stress the necessary singularity of ideas to form a cohesive community, are most open to this criticism. Such theories argue that the equality-efficiency dilemma is an insoluble problem of liberal democracy because there is no way to weigh the value of each objective (MacIntyre 1988; Bellah et al. 1985). But when the community rather than the individual determines value, alternate objectives may be readily compared. If the community believes that the problem of sustainable development requires a substantial communal response, the primacy of community rights over individual rights will permit a more effective response. A moral community would more readily be able to accept and distribute any necessary suffering in order that it might sustain its development. A communal response led by the agency of government could readily bring a shift to an environmental techno-economic paradigm. But at what cost in economic efficiency and personal liberty?

Tradition and culture, if they are effective in maintaining community, are relatively inflexible. They create community by providing a common and consistent set of beliefs and values upon which individuals draw. Community is constructed from these similarly constituted individuals as they are constructed from the community's common beliefs and values. The more that individual and communal identity are defined by historically constructed tradition, the greater the probability that the group will be intolerant of new ideas. If a community seeks to cement its self-identity by returning to earlier patterns of social relations, it will prefer conservation of past political and social institutions, substantially diminishing its capacity for social change. It may be unable to adapt its social order to the demands of sustainable development. Hard communitarians, far from seeking to explain how beliefs and values can change, seek to implement institutions that prevent change, ensuring that common values and beliefs are passed down the generations.

It is unclear how a community so constituted would be able to adapt to uncertain but real ecological limits. A community that totally constitutes its members through a common moral code or cultural tradition limits individual choices and creativeness. The very holism of community may prevent a plurality of ideas necessary to find solutions to the many subproblems of sustainable development. Just as markets seem to encourage innovation, enhancing individual freedom may enhance policy creativity and communal flexibility.

The liberal community also can lead to intolerance and authoritarian rule, for "insofar as our public life has withered, our sense of common involvement diminished, to that extent we lie vulnerable to the mass politics of totalitarian solutions" (Sandel, quoted in d'Entrèves 1990, 85). Liberalism imagines individuals who are free of or "outside" society. How can a society of such individuals act in the public interest? If individuals are pursuing their own projects, they will not act for the public interest where they do not believe it to be in their personal interest—which is usually short-term, as demonstrated by consumers' high discount rate. Increasing equity and political participation will not necessarily encourage individual self-seekers to incorporate community interests in their personal projects. Thus, when a vital public interest such as sustainable development exists, it must be imposed by government in the name of the community. However, if individuals are not wholly selfish but are concerned about 'the other' and may even have and recognize duties to others, they will still be able to adapt communally.

"Soft" communitarian ideas specify a self that is reflective and can rationally deliberate. They loosen the bonds of community, allowing for a plurality of values within the community without resulting in the anomie of liberal modernity. A debate within a community to which individuals consciously belong can reconcile different values. Without some sense of the common good, "pluralism is merely the multiplication of points of intolerance" (Hendley 1993, 310). The "sense of the common good" permits a pluralism of ideas while constraining potentially destructive competition within liberalism. In practical terms, this sense of the common good is little different from the "self-restraint" assumed in classical liberalism or the 'consideration of the other' embedded in most contemporary liberal theory. As there is a threat of what Foucault calls "docility," approximately a passive acceptance of structures, in *both* liberal and communitarian societies (Kateb 1989; Foucault 1977), a continual realignment of political institutions would be necessary.

Similarities between soft communitarianism and contemporary liberalism offer hope for a new model of politics to reduce the tension between the needs of individuals and the collective. I discuss such a model of discursive politics after first considering, in the next section, the dominant rational choice methodology of political science that is based in positivist libertarian political theory.

POLITICS AS RATIONAL CHOICE

In contrast to the normative discussion in political theory and in the optimistic model of politics discussed in the next section, most theorizing in political science has been determinedly positivist and pessimistic. There are many rational choice theories but they all reflect "the economic study of non-market decision making, or simply the application of economics to political science" (Mueller 1989, 1). Thus, politics is viewed as a marketplace of ideas in which political consumers choose those ideas that benefit themselves. As in the economic market, power inequalities (often the result of financial inequalities produced in the economy) affect outcomes.

These theories offer a systematic analysis of political realities using "deductive accounts of incentives, constraints and calculations that confront individuals" (Green and Shapiro 1994, 3). They assume that each individual maximizes the expected values of her payoffs; that individuals are the relevant maximizers; that rationality is consistency and transitive preferences; and that these rules apply to all people at all times. Individual actions are based on desires and interests that themselves grow out of personal beliefs. Beliefs and desires are consistent and rationally pursued—"the agent must not act on a desire that, in his own opinion, is less weighty than other desires which are reasons for not performing the action" (Elster 1986, 16). Actions are "caused" by beliefs and desires such that the effect is as the agent desired. Individuals are seen as pursuing their self-interest, internally determined in a logical and consistent manner. Social and cultural effects on individual decision making are, in practice, ignored (Green and Shapiro 1994, 14–17). Governance is seen as a process of "muddling through," making marginal policy changes from a complex process of discovering the lowest common denominator between opposing group interests (Lindblom 1959 and 1980).

The stature of these theories rests on the explicitly scientific rational choice research program. In the manner of the physical sciences, rational choice theorists hope to discover internally consistent, logical, empirically testable theories that are descriptive, explanatory, *and* predictive. Because of these ambitious scientific goals, much rational choice empirical work has focused on political behavior restricted in time and place (such as voter or legislative behavior) where variables are more limited and necessary simplifying assumptions appear most realistic (Green and Shapiro 1994). Yet, by its own measures of success, rational choice has underperformed. Although it is avowedly empirical, for a number of reasons both theoretical and methodological, it has failed to provide more than minimal empirical support for its hypotheses (Green and Shapiro 1994; Monroe 1993; Petracca 1991).

Even if rational choice theories were able to explain short-term, limited political behavior, for four reasons they would be unlikely to either explain or encourage an effective politics of sustainable development. First, rational choice has not been able to successfully explain the rapid, widespread growth in environmental legislation. In all industrial and some developing countries there has been action to reduce destruction of the natural environment despite entrenched industrial resistance to regulation. As a rational choice theorist admits: "Around 1970 and again since 1988, the normal events of producer-group bargaining have been upset by an unexpected surge of environmentalism among voters. Exactly why remains a mystery" (McLean 1991). Probably many people's desires changed; acting rationally on a new desire their political behaviors changed (Inglehart 1990 purports to measure this shift in desires in the rich countries).

Second, if desires (or "preferences") are socially, culturally, or institutionally constructed, they may diverge substantially across countries and regions within countries, especially with respect to issues as emotive as environment and development. To simplify model building and to satisfy the scientific demand for parsimony, rational choice theorists assume that although the appropriate unit of analysis is the individual, desires are similar among all individuals and over time. However, social and cultural factors affect desires, and political institutions change the behaviors that are rational in the pursuit of those desires much as market structures influence economic activity. Thus, differences between societies prevent rational choice theory from achieving its goal of a meaningful universal explanation of political behavior.

Third, the utility maximization assumption may not reflect individual behavior. The behavior of individuals in small groups faced with common pool resource problems more closely resembles satisficing (e.g., Ostrom et al. 1994 among others; Simon 1972). Indeed, it often is not possible for individuals to determine what maximization means. Corporations, which are probably more rational than most individuals, usually aim for specified targets for return on investment and other financial measures. Though they hope to exceed these targets, they are satisfied if they meet them.

Finally, if political actors believe that rational choice theories do generally explain political behavior, joint action in pursuit of sustainable development within political communities will be less possible. Desires become limited by expectations of limited outcomes: "Taking a preference for the maximization of self-interest or even utility as a given begets both a cognitive and a political reality in which individuals and political leaders alike come to view such behavior as normatively acceptable and as the standard by which government should operate" (Petracca 1991, 313–314). Rational choice theory "preserves the *status quo*" and "public policy *as is* becomes the public policy interest as it *ought to be*" [emphasis in original] and political actors learn that only pursuit of self-interest is politically successful. Thus, rational choice theories corrode the necessary connections between individuals that make possible communal action in response to a common threat. If these theories are a reasonable representation of political reality, there is little hope for sustainable development. A belief that they are an accurate representation of reality would block collective action to avoid exceeding ecological limits.

## DISCURSIVE POLITICS

Through an analysis of U.S. political activity, Stone (1988) heaps scorn on rational policy models. She proposes what I shall call "discursive politics" as an optimistic positivist model of U.S. political activity that combines elements of self-restrained modern liberalism and soft communitarian thought. Informed by feminist and postmodernist ideas, this discursive politics emphasizes the connectedness between members of the community that prevents decision-making breakdown and develops consensual processes. Far from being ahistorical and asocial self-seekers, individuals are viewed as influenced by the culture and society in which they are embedded. Citizenship is more than self-interest: humans are social animals before they are citizens. Beliefs and values that are socially influenced are formed before the self that has interests and affect the individual choice of interests.

The political community, or *polis*, is not a market; it is a community in which individuals and groups discourse over ideas—"the very stuff of politics" (Stone 1988, 25). This discourse is influenced by beliefs about the way the world works and values about what is individually and socially good: "political conflict is never simply over material conditions and choices but over what is legitimate." This is a continuing process: "problems in the *polis* are never 'solved' in the way that economic needs are met in the market model." Democracy is not only a means for totting up the personal preferences of voters, formed elsewhere in personal projects and interests or in culturally founded beliefs. Democracy is a discourse about communal projects, it is about the participation of members of the polis in the process of forming and disseminating ideas. So, this approach inquires into the process by which political preferences are formed more than about the mere counting of those preferences.

Stone lists ten characteristics of the polis: it is a community with a public interest in which most policy problems are commons problems, cooperation is more prevalent than competition, and loyalty is the norm. Information is interpretive, incomplete, and strategic, and the polis is governed by the laws of passion "as well as the laws of matter." Power that is derived from all these elements "coordinates individual intentions and actions into collective purposes and results" (Stone 1988:25). In nearly every respect this view of the process of politics is completely opposed to rational choice political science theories, as "the influence of values, ethics, and ideas on individual motivation are alien to rational choice theories of human nature" (Petracca 1991).

An essential part of the discursive political process is participation. To be legitimate, political discourse demands equal participation within the political community. Equal participation is a goal of liberals, radicals, and communitarians. Greater participation in decision making is both more necessary and more likely in a liberal society. The discursive approach to politics presumes that the community wields influence over participants, pressing them toward some common action that may not be in every (or any) participant's individual self-interest. Thus, Stone emphasizes the cooperation, passion, and community of politics in the polis.

Stone's analysis shows that the belonging engendered by culture, shared traditions, and social relations in the polis enriches the lives of its members. The public interest is not an objective calculation; it is socially constructed through relations in the polis: it lives within the political community and is an emanation from it. It is not a fixed goal; it is the continual product of a continuous process by which contending interpretations of events and data are compared and reworked within a community context. Whatever the differences in personal goals, in beliefs and values, common membership in a community leads to acceptable compromises and away from an intractable conflict of interests. From the liberal perspective, the causation works the other way: greater equity leads to more participation and, thus, to a sense of community.[11] If, as argued in chapter 2, scientific knowledge is insufficient to be a basis of action, problems cannot be clearly identified and efficient and effective solutions objectively selected.[12] Optimization then must be measured in the *process* of discoursing about possible solutions and socially constructing reality rather than in the outcome. Without an objective measure of the net benefits from alternate solutions, emphasis on equality of participation adds value to the process by increasing equity without degrading the outcome of the process.

## THE ECOLOGICAL USES OF POLITICS

The discursive politics approach does not explain how development will be sustained through political institutions. However, its image of a continual discourse within a communal political process is certainly more optimistic than a rational choice politics of self. The continuous interplay of ideas allows policy to change as a result of rhetorical discourse, discourse that combines facts with their interpretation through values and beliefs. If there is a generally equal ability of all participants to influence the outcome, discourse over collective action may not result in objectively optimal policies but will satisfy one component of sustainable development, equity in collective choice.

The realization of community should encourage the polis to concentrate on what its members can agree on. Differences in values can be explicitly recognized for what they are—subjective differences in valuing aspects of the world. An understanding of the need for some collective action in environmental issues encourages the seeking of common ground.

For example, in the Rocky Mountain West, environmentalists and ranchers have found they can agree on policies to preserve open spaces and other characteristics of the mountain environment once they explicitly recognize their value differences.[13] They may never solve the problem but they continue to work on it. As sustainable development is not a problem with a definition and a solution, it is entirely appropriate that, as Stone notes, collective problems are rarely solved in the polis. But the polis shows how discourse can be maintained, while more conservative rational choice political models cannot.

# 6

## SUSTAINABILITY IN THE INTERNATIONAL SYSTEM

Development may be unsustainable at the local, national, regional, or global level. All development occurs within the context of a local ecosystem, individual local and national cultures, distinct political structures, economic capabilities, and natural endowments. But development of local communities—countries, cities, towns, villages, and so forth—must be sustained within global ecosystems, a global economy, and an international political system. International cooperation will be necessary to address global and regional aspects of sustainable development and many local problems.

In the equity policy narrative, re-allocation of power over natural goods is a priority in sustaining development. Resulting from an accumulation of historical events including war and colonial and economic exploitation, the distribution of economic and political power in the international system is inequitable and inhibits LDC development.[1] The equity narrative implies that sustainable development will also require amelioration of the grossest international inequities, probably including structural change. Any structural change presupposes international cooperation.[2]

International relations (IR) theorists have not attempted to explain how countries, states, and localities might cooperate to sustain development, nor have they speculated on the order and structure of the international system that might promote global sustainable development.[3] That is the purpose of this chapter. The first section assesses the nature of the interaction between the international system and unsustainability at the local and global levels. International political and economic structures that create local problems of unsustainability and abuse of global common-pool resources result from insufficient international political cooperation. The second section considers the effect of global political and economic structures on the sustainable development policy choices available to countries and their sub-units. The third section considers the possibility of cooperation between countries to ameliorate global environmental problems.[4] Many scholars predict that because states seek power over other states in an anarchic international system, they will be unable to cooperate effectively to preserve global commons or provide public goods.[5] Other scholars believe that international institutions may modify states' interests to encourage international cooperation and global governance. Still other scholars argue that international cooperation in environmental issues results from the common beliefs of a small group of scientific or technical experts or from the interaction of knowledge and power.

The fourth section considers three mechanisms that might reduce the ability of the international political system and of economic structures to inhibit sustainable development around the world. It is possible that a global civil society acting from the grass-roots level may produce convergence between states' preferences. Additionally, international institutions may ameliorate some of the worst effects of global economic systems by encouraging technology transfer and development aid flows. Finally, a sense of community between states may create shared values that will enhance meaningful cooperation on intransigent issues such as the North-South divide and economic sovereignty. A concluding section discusses the probability of effective change in global structures and an increase in global cooperation.

## LEVELS OF ANALYSIS

The international system comprises countries, states, international and domestic organizations, domestic polities, groups, and individuals. The actions of any international actor may affect any other international actor. Actions and events at one level of analysis may create effects at another.

A 'global' cause or effect is one that is widely distributed around the world such that every locale contributes to it or is affected by it, though perhaps to different degrees. For the present purposes it is sufficient to include within the term *local* the country together with all its political sub-units: state, city, county, town, village, socio-economic group, and so on. As sustainable development is a primarily anthropocentric term, effects of human choices on ecosystems wholly or largely within a country are important to the extent they may, in turn, restrain its human development. Local events with local effects will include deforestation

**Table 2**

Levels of Analysis

| Locus of Effect | Locus of Cause | Example | Locus of Solution |
|---|---|---|---|
| Local | Local | Deforestation for fuel; ground-level ozone, CO and $CO_2$; consumer culture; elite government | Local |
| Local | Regional, international | Acid rain; international river basins | International |
| Global | Global | Stratospheric ozone depletion; climate change | International |
| Local | Global | Technology; global markets | State and international |

for fuel in LDCs and ground-level ozone produced by traffic in cities in industrialized countries. It will also include cultural and social causes and effects such as land tenure systems, government regulation, and consumerism. The problem of effects in one geographical locale or social group within a country as a result of activity in another locale or group, while very real and contentious, may be addressed by governments at one or more levels within the country. This chapter is concerned with causes that have effects on political units or eco-systems in one or more countries. Table 2 outlines the types of global-local cause-effect linkages of interest.

The regional-local connection is exemplified by cross-border resource depletion, or more commonly, pollution flows. International law holds countries responsible for the environmental harms their emissions cause to other countries.[6] International cooperation, aided by international institutions, has created management of many such cross-border environmental problems as acid rain in Europe and the Rhine River (Bernauer and Moser 1996; Levy 1993). The close proximity and small number of countries make regional environmental problems more manageable than those with global causes or effects. However, their solution is usually comparable in nature to that sought in global-global problems.

Stratospheric ozone depletion and climate change are examples of global causes with global effects. Both the causes of each problem and their effects are distributed across the globe.[7] Ozone-depleting substances

(ODSs) are emitted from a wide range of industrial activities located around the world. Nearly every human activity—from rice growing and forest clearing for grazing lands to manufacturing and transportation—causes increases in atmospheric concentrations of GHGs.[8]

## GLOBAL STRUCTURES

Rapidly evolving global economic structures significantly influence local policy choices in two ways. First, global markets for manufactured products, raw materials, and food make natural goods usage in one country reflect consumption choices in other countries.[9] Quality and safety standards in the principal food-consuming countries dictate agricultural practices in food-producing countries. Highly polluting support industries (such as fertilizer, herbicide, and pesticide production) follow the agricultural practices from the rich to the poor countries, sometimes with disastrous results. Transnational corporations (TNCs) aid in this expropriation of natural goods from poor countries by rich countries.

Second, technology developed in industrialized countries to reflect their consumption needs and resource and capital endowments usually becomes the standard to be applied everywhere. The Union Carbide plant that exploded in Bhopal in 1984 was comparable to plants in the United States, one of which only months later accidentally released toxic fumes requiring the evacuation of the local residents. Chemical plants have polluted local communities from New York State to Seveso in Italy (World Commission on Environment and Development 1987, 228–229; *World Resources 1996–97*, 15). Refineries, power plants, and steel mills use similar technology the world over with similar damage to local environments, although emissions controls are usually more stringent and more effective in industrialized countries.[10] As new technology is introduced in industrialized countries, older, more polluting, and less energy-efficient technology is sold to the LDCs. With the lower labor and higher capital costs in those countries, less than optimally eco-efficient second-hand technology finds a new lease on life (Pack 1985).

In both cases, the influence of global structures is felt in local ecosystems and thence in many human populations dispersed globally. Resources are exploited wherever they occur to satisfy global demand. The successful model of Japan and the Four Tigers has made export-led industrialization the accepted economic development model among LDC policy elites. However, LDCs have little choice, as the global market forces all producers to satisfy the same product quality, requiring comparable techniques everywhere.[11]

Interdependence, especially assymetrical interdependence, reduces the ability of states to regulate the domestic effects of global political economic structures (Keohane and Nye 1989; Cooper 1968). Smaller and poorer countries have fewer policy tools to protect themselves against damaging dependence on larger and richer countries. Particularly in LDCs but to some extent everywhere, local policies are unable to prevent incursions from global structures or to prevent their excessive consumption of local natural goods. However, there is no more support today among the industrialized countries for international policies to restrain the globalization of markets or their effects within individual countries than there was for a New International Economic Order a quarter century ago.[12] While some international policy has been created to limit the global effects of globally caused environmental problems, no policy to reduce the negative local effects of global structures is likely in the foreseeable future.

Reducing the inequities in international structures could contribute to sustainable development in three ways. First, very poor countries are unable to acquire or use the most eco-efficient technologies. As poor countries industrialize, consumption of natural goods should increase. Raising LDC wealth closer to that of the rich countries would restrain natural goods consumption increases. Second, if sustainable development implies a greater equity between individuals within a country, it also must between countries. The Brundtland Commission (World Commission 1987) argued that equity between generations implies equity within generations (across borders). Last, it is probable that developing countries will actively seek to conserve local and global natural goods as they get richer and to participate in international cooperation to sustain development if they see themselves as more equal partners with the rich countries.

In the absence of international cooperation to restrain the globalization of markets or their ecological effects, education of consumers in rich countries and of producers everywhere might reduce local environmental damage.[13] However, LDCs seek technology for economic growth and the older, less eco-efficient technologies use more labor, the most abundant factor of production in many LDCs (Bhalla and Dilmus 1988; Bhalla 1985). The industrialized countries also have consistently rejected transfers of the most eco-efficient technologies at less-than-market prices, citing a need to protect the value of patents and copyrights in order to encourage technological innovation.[14]

## COOPERATION BETWEEN SOVEREIGNTIES

International cooperation is a slippery concept. Among the many definitions, Keohane (1984, 51) offers one of the more widely accepted: cooperation "requires that the action of separate individuals or organizations—which are not in pre-existent harmony—be brought into conformity with one another through a process of policy coordination." In the context of this book, international cooperation might be thought of as the result of a process of interaction between countries through which the participants agree to change their behaviors as part of a global effort to sustain development.

Power-based theories—historically dominant among IR theories—assume that each country seeks relative power (political, economic, and primarily military) over other countries in order to defend its territory and thus enhance the prosperity of its citizens (Vasquez 1983; Carr 1951; Morgenthau 1978). While realism offers a compelling and parsimonious explanation of the self-protection behavior of countries, a belief in the veracity of such theories tends to reduce the desire for, or expectation of, cooperation as a solution to international problems. Just as the market reduces trust (Hodgson 1994), breaking down social ties, realist theory anticipates self-interested behavior and insists that states must rely on self-help only. Neither allies, other states, nor international organizations should be expected to act except to benefit themselves; and if the state may not count on others to help protect it, security lies in dominance over others (Gilpin 1981 and 1984). Power-based theories offer no explanation for the international cooperation that has occurred in a number of global and international environmental issues and suggests no international system aid to global sustainable development. More useful theoretical approaches include interests and knowledge-based theories of international cooperation.

## Interests

Recent liberal theorizing has argued that in many issue areas states seek absolute power—power to achieve some desired objective—rather than relative power *over* other states (Grieco 1988). States seek power *to* achieve some subjective goals, their "interests." These interests extend beyond territorial integrity, survival of the state, and protection of the people, to economic and sometimes even moral goals.

States act within a network of international institutions that are "persistent and connected sets of rules and practices that prescribe behavioral roles, constrain activity, and shape expectations" (Keohane et al. 1993). These include legislative and customary law, accepted diplomatic practices, treaty-based regimes and conventions, and international organizations with independent budgets and defined missions. "Neoliberal institutionalist" theories argue that international institutions[15] modify the behaviors of rational self-seeking states by changing their calculations of interests and expectations of payoffs to actions. Institutions influence the "understandings that leaders of states have of the roles they should play and their assumptions about others' motivations and perceived self-interests" (Keohane 1989, 6).

Although the process of institution formation generally is expected to reflect realities of power, once formed, institutions take on a life of their own. They are "frozen rules" that "prescribe behavioral roles, constrain activity, and shape expectations" (Keohane et al. 1993, 5). They offer "an environment in which socialization and learning can occur ... [and] provide information, increase trust, and reduce uncertainty about the actions of others" (Caporaso 1992, 625), thus enhancing the probability of cooperation (Keohane 1989; Young 1989a).

Because they inhibit radical changes in the power structure in the issue area (Keohane 1984) and because states generally pursue short-term gains, institutions may prevent changes necessary to permit all countries to sustain development. If they are not to become a force opposing real and necessary change in the international system, institutions must acquire some degree of autonomy. As the members control international organizations and define institutions, the developed countries are often able to prevent changes, as in capital or trade flows, that would primarily benefit developing countries. However, in some international environmental treaties LDCs have been able to wring concessions from the industrialized countries (Miller 1995).

States are expected to calculate their interests in terms of objective factors such as the cost of pollution mitigation or the benefit to a state of the harm reduction from an international regulatory regime (Sprinz and Vaahtoranta 1994; Saetevik 1988). Domestic political factors as suggested by Putnam (1988) are rarely included in assessments of interests or systematically studied. In reality they are very important and sometimes critical to states' preferences for outcomes of international cooperation (Harrison 1994).

Because the concept of "interests" is so devalued by common misuse and by theoretical confusion, it is better represented by the notion of preferences. States may not be able clearly to define their interests but they usually are able to order possible outcomes and the actions that might bring them about. Although sustainable development may be in the interest of each country, the absence of any objective or agreed definition means that the concept cannot be used as an "interest" to drive state policy choices in the international arena.[16]

Outcome preferences are comparable to what Goldstein and Keohane (1993, 9) have called "principled beliefs": "normative ideas that specify criteria for distinguishing right from wrong and just from unjust."

Action preferences result from causal beliefs "about cause-effect relation-ships which derive authority from the shared consensus of recognized elites . . . they imply strategies for the attainment of goals themselves valued because of shared principled beliefs." They include scientific knowledge and experience-derived knowledge of the actions of other countries. States pursue valued ends by selecting strategies for action designed in accordance with their contingent understanding of the world. States may pursue outcome preferences such as peace, prosperity, human rights, and justice in any number of ways depending on their under-standing of the context.

Models of international behavior optimized for security issues ignore an essential question: *What do states value in the environmental issue area?*[17] Most international relations theories, especially structural theories, assume the state's preferences over outcomes and then attempt to ex-plain states' actions (Powell 1994). This approach is appropriate when preferences over outcomes are relatively invariable or objectively pre-dictable (as in security issues) and the actions that might produce those outcomes well understood. However, sustainable development presents states with greater problems of preference ordering than other issues. States are always uncertain about which actions will achieve their out-come preferences because of *strategic* uncertainty about the attributes and preferences of other states (Iida 1993). They can assign subjective prob-abilities to the likely responses of other states, the quality of which im-proves with repeated observation of comparable events, improving the probability of cooperation through multiple interactions.[18] However, per-formance in trade negotiations, for example, will not necessarily be a predictor of behavior in the environmental negotiations that would be part of sustaining development through the international system.[19]

Sustainable development also presents states with a significant problem of *analytic* uncertainty, states' uncertainty about their own pay-offs from accepting any international policy (Iida 1993). Over a long pe-riod of steadily reducing tariffs from successive rounds of negotiations under the rules of the General Agreement on Tariffs and Trade, states have learned the effects on their economies of tariff reductions. However, in the absence of scientific knowledge, analytic uncertainty about sustainable development can only be lessened by evidence of potentially irreversible and catastrophic changes in the health of the ecological systems that sup-port human life and wellbeing. Continuing analytic uncertainty makes strategic uncertainty unstable, if country behaviors are assumed to be based on rational payoff calculations. States will be unable to predict ac-tion and response by other states, and their subjective probability assess-ments of others' payoffs will continually vary even if they are accurate.

Young (1989b) argues that what he calls the "veil of uncertainty" *contributes* to cooperation. Analogously to Rawls' "veil of ignorance," uncertainty prevents rational calculation from being exclusively self-interested. If states are unable to assess the costs and benefits to them of agreeing to international rules, they will choose rules that are fairer; unable to seek individual maximization, they should, Young argues, seek equity. That is, under conditions of uncertainty about the outcomes of specific behaviors, states should prefer internationally equitable remedies. There is little evidence that this is occurring—perhaps because states have not yet realized how uncertain they are about sustainable development. As long as sustainable development is understood as a vague idea rather than a pressing problem, the inherent analytical uncertainty in the concept is hidden, and equitable international remedies will not be preferred by states.

## Knowledge

Although science may not be able to define sustainable development and offer a clear path to it, it will be important in both local and global policy. Scientific knowledge and scientific experts may be expected to influence states' understanding of sustainable and unsustainable development and their outcome and action preferences. However, scientific knowledge is not independent of social structures. Especially when scientific data are incomplete or when there is disagreement over data interpretation, meanings ascribed to scientific data are connected to social and political relations. "Epistemic communities" of like-minded technical experts that interpret ambiguous or incomplete data in accordance with their values have been identified in a number of international environmental issues as playing a substantial role in state preference formation. A transnational epistemic community is able to influence international policy through the instrumental use of knowledge that, because of uncertain data, they have been able to define through their values (Haas 1990 and 1992b). Through its members' influence in domestic decision-making, the community should be able to coordinate the domestic policies of many states. However, it is rarely possible to demonstrate a clear influence by an identifiable epistemic community on state behaviors (Shackley and Wynne 1995 and 1996; Haas 1990 and 1992a, Harrison 1998).

Because of the wide range of sciences involved in understanding sustainable development, it is unlikely that an epistemic community of scientists will arise. However, each of the three narratives discussed in this book has been advanced in some form by scholars and others who share values, beliefs, and political purposes. Because its message of laissez-faire accords with the prevailing ideology,[20] the efficiency narrative has had most influence over states' preference orderings, principally as a default position. Neither of the other narratives has gathered anything resembling an epistemic community, although the equity narrative was advanced by the Brundtland Commission.

As Foucault (1980) argues and Bacon before him, scientific "knowledge" imbues its possessor with power. Thus, power and knowledge can be seen as mutually constitutive. Politically powerful countries are able to define scientific knowledge in accordance with their interests. Knowledge grows out of a discourse between different rhetorical positions, with the more powerful participants having more influence on the final socially (and politically) constructed knowledge (Litfin 1994). Power is related to structure, both of the social system and the process, and knowledge becomes what the community accepts.

If this interpretation of international environmental politics is correct, the politically powerful countries—the developed countries—would be able to define sustainable development globally and, through the international system, largely dictate how LDCs will understand and respond to unsustainability. Past history and modern conceptions of self-interested sovereignties suggest that developed countries will attempt to sustain their own development by exporting social dislocation to LDCs and avoiding it at home.[21] In the climate change negotiations, the developed countries have pressured developing countries, in the name of global efficiency, to permit the majority of mitigation measures to be pursued in developing countries using developed country technology.[22] The availability of a lower-cost solution has prevented the United States and some other developed states from acting in accordance with the equity principle in the UNFCCC.

OPPORTUNITIES FOR COOPERATION

So far, this review of the principal theoretical approaches to international relations has revealed a low probability that the international system will foster global sustainable development. However, theoretical analyses do suggest three ways in which this goal may be achieved. First, issue linkage and multilateralism may modify the dominant self-interested behavior of states. Second, socialization of states may permit principles of equity to be more widely accepted by states. Third, development of a global civil society may marginalize (or lead) international political processes, lessening their constraints on global sustainable development.

## Multilateralism

As in other international environmental issues, sustainable development should attract more issue-linkage strategies than most other issues in international relations (Haas 1980 and 1983) and foster multilateralism (Ruggie 1993).[23] The breadth of the issues encompassed in sustainable development creates myriad issue-linkage opportunities. However, the complexity of trade-offs across multiple issues and between multiple countries is likely to hinder any international agreement. Because multilateral negotiations concern commons issues of uncertain cost, there is less reason for states to treat the negotiations as zero-sum (Ruggie 1992). Agreements would result from bargaining among all participating states as a result of principled behavior rather than rent-seeking.[24] Young's (1989b) suggestion that "fairness" rules under uncertainty is an example of this more generalized principled behavior.

## Socialization

There is limited evidence that the international system "socializes" states, affecting what they believe is fair and just action and modifying their preferences. This "reflectivist" (Keohane 1988) or "constructivist" (Wendt 1987) analysis argues that agents cannot be separated from the social systems they inhabit. Preferences depend upon cognition of the world; how a state "perceives" the world influences its preference over both outcomes and actions. Cognitions may change through adaptation or learning.[25] Countries may learn from each other within an international institutional framework and adapt to international institutional agreements, aided by the information gathering and dissemination functions of intergovernmental organizations (Keohane 1983). Interaction between states within a socializing international system may change both their principled and causal beliefs and their outcome and action preferences.

Constructivist approaches assert that actor identities are "relatively stable, role specific understandings and expectations about self" that precede interests and "are inherently relational" (Wendt 1992).[26] Because "people act toward objects, including other actors, on the basis of the meaning that the objects have for them" and because meaning is not independent of social context, individual "identities and . . . collective cognitions [institutions] do not exist apart from each other; they are 'mutually constitutive.' " Agents both construct and are constructed by social institutions, which are "collective meanings that constitute the structures which organize our actions." States' preferences will be modified by the institutions they form. If those institutions have individual life—an ability to transform themselves to adapt to systemic needs rather than power distributions—they could encourage equitable international behavior in states' preference orderings.

## Civil Society

Environmental nongovernmental organizations (ENGOs) are a significant part of environmental learning at all levels of society (Wapner 1996; Lipschutz 1996; McCormick 1989; Princen and Finger 1994). Their rhetoric is usually explicitly value laden, reflecting the ethical orientation discussed in detail in chapter 7. At the local level, ENGOs influence the preferences of groups that may act directly to sustain development or may pressure local governments to pursue appropriate policies. Simultaneously, globalization of communications and increasing travel and other interaction between the peoples of different countries may be globalizing civil society. Because the Internet, the World Wide Web, ENGOs, and green parties help to disseminate ideas and publicize successful local policies, they may subvert or diminish the value of international processes.[27] Despite the rhetoric of sustainable development as a global problem and the evident global socio-economic linkages, opportunities abound for local responses and for grassroots pressure for behavioral changes. Some analysts (Lipschutz 1996; Wapner 1996) have already identified such local pressures for environmental action on a global scale. Others (Princen and Finger 1994; Keohane and Nye 1989) point to the increasing but opposed influences of ENGOs and transnational corporations on states and directly on international processes.[28]

ENGOs also directly influence international processes. They often act collectively in international negotiations, educating delegates about their proposals and disseminating relevant data.[29] For example, the "precautionary principle," a mantra of the environmental movement, has been included in some international environmental treaties such as the UNFCCC. This principle requires that states act to mediate anthropogenic damage to ecological systems before scientific evidence of deterioration is available. As a principle for state behaviors, it is at present honored more in the breach, but its consistent restatement may progressively affect states' preferences.

### CONCLUSION

The World Commission on Environment and Development concluded optimistically that extended powers for the United Nations would go a long way to sustaining development (World Commission 1987, 308–347). This book demurs. Sustainable development requires much more than international cooperation fostered by "institutional and legal changes" and expanding the powers of intergovernmental organizations.[30] Even within the international system, development cannot be sustained merely by multiplying international institutions. Institutions may help to sustain development (or at least reduce hindrances in the international system) if they are flexible, if they are inclusive, if they reduce the inequities in international structures, and if they lead to changes in the ideas and beliefs held by states and their leaders—none of which can be guaranteed by their existence alone.

Despite the globalization of markets and the apparent development of a global civil society, states continue to dominate decisions about an equitable distribution of the costs and benefits of sustainable development. However, much of international relations theory is of no value in predicting how states in an anarchic international system will be able to sustain development globally, especially if that requires an equitable distribution of the costs and benefits of sustainable development. Power-based theories are irrelevant; a sustainable world is not a world of *realpolitik* states. Because sustainable development cannot be objectively defined and because the relevant cause-effect relations are uncertain, states' outcome and action preferences will be vague and varying. Because of the nature of sustainable development, it is improbable that epistemic communities will coordinate countries' policies. The power that scientific knowledge grants primarily to the developed states may actually inhibit the necessary changes in the international system. Simultaneously, the paucity of relevant scientific knowledge prevents any serious debate over international sustainable development policy.

Once sustainable development emerges as an important issue on the international agenda and becomes more real than vague words, progress may be possible. Uncertainty about the consequences of actions may pressure states to prefer equitable solutions, with multilateralism resulting. Through social interaction, states may come to understand sustainable development as a problem that will require a more equitable international system for its solution. Despite the claims of some critics in the developed world, there is little evidence that the evolving global market benefits developing countries at the expense of the developed world.[31] It will require a massive and long-term effort of global cooperation for a more equitable international economic order to replace the global political economic structures that primarily benefit the developed countries. This is unlikely.

Finally, a developing global civil society could pressure states to change their preferences and policies. Environmental activist groups and ENGOs may encourage localized sustainable development policy and practice and undermine states' monopoly of the issue, pressuring states to cooperate internationally to preserve their influence. Perhaps only by threatening the dominance of the international system can development be sustained globally.

# 7

## A PROBLEM OF CONSCIOUSNESS

Both the efficiency and equity narratives are facets of "environmentalism." The principal concerns of environmentalism are "(1) the preservation of wilderness, endangered species, and wildlife habitat; (2) pollution; (3) the availability of nonrenewable mineral resources; (4) the ability to produce enough food for everyone; (5) the long-term adequacy of energy supplies; and (6) the threat of war in a nuclear age" (Paehlke 1989, 113). These are all legitimate *instrumental* values—valued because of the benefits they would confer on humanity. "Nature" and human systems transact and actions and outcomes are judged in anthropocentric terms. Paehlke lists thirteen core values of environmentalism, all of which may reasonably be considered desirable social improvements absent any conservation or preservation of ecosystems.

The ethics narrative reflects the holistic, systemic logic of ecology, that humans are an integral part of a single system of nature or of life and have no hierarchical position over nonhumans.[1] No longer can humans choose actions toward nature that are only good *for them*; in some sense they must be good for the whole that only *includes* humans.[2] This narrative completely restates the problem as one of the health of the systemic whole greater than the needs of humanity alone. In doing so, it redefines sustainable development and implies policies very different from those proposed by the other narratives. By emphasizing the interrelations of humanity to its nonhuman surroundings, the various green theories within this policy narrative invoke new ideas of value, of rights, of ethics, and of human self-actualization (Bellah et al. 1985, 284–286; Toulmin 1982, 228–234). This narrative rejects the belief that the environment can be managed[3] to satisfy human needs "without fundamental changes in present values or patterns of production and consumption"

81

(Dobson 1995, 1).[4] It substitutes the idea that "a sustainable and fulfilling existence pre-supposes radical changes in our relationship with the non-human natural world, and in our mode of social and political life."

Sustainable development describes a relationship between human development and nonhuman ecosystems. For many theorists and activists, development can only be sustained through an ethic that recognizes a fundamental equality between humans and nonhumans.[5] Many analytical approaches propose different visions of this goal. This chapter reviews these approaches to identify the commonalities of their policy proposals.

One approach proposes an extension of legal rights from humans to nonhuman life. Legally equitable processes that are inclusive of nonhumans would, it is supposed, lead to a sustainable relationship between humanity and the rest of the natural world. A second approach asserts a direct linkage between the quality of relations between humans and the quality of relations between the human and nonhuman systems. Faults in one relationship are reflected in the other. A third approach argues that for humans to appropriately consider nonhumans, they must separate the valuation of nonhumans from their human uses. A final approach emphasizes the importance, for human self-actualization, of individual human relations to the natural environment requiring a spiritual or quasi-religious experience of connectedness to nature. A section of this chapter is devoted to each approach.

The penultimate section synthesizes them and draws out their common policy implications. Whereas the other sustainable development policy narratives assume that sustainable development will result from institutional changes, the ethics policy narrative assumes that sustainable development can only be achieved through a revolution in the ideas carried in the minds of men and women. Human behaviors can be modified through institutionally applied incentives and disincentives, a Pavlovian approach assumed in the efficiency and equity narratives. Or humans can choose to change their behavior because of a change in their beliefs and values, or a change in their understanding of cause-effect relations. Thus, policies emanating from this narrative revolve around human learning and the means to encourage it. However, none of the theories discussed here defines a practical path to their shared goal. Primarily concerned with describing the end, they overlook the problem of means. Because these theories are concerned to maintain individual freedom to choose one's ideas, they do not support organized political action. A concluding section summarizes what can be learned from the ethics narrative for policy for sustainable development.

## EXTENDING LEGAL RIGHTS

In 1970, Walt Disney obtained a permit from the U.S. Forest Service to construct a resort in the hitherto undeveloped Mineral King Valley in the Sierra Nevada Mountains in California. Various environmental organizations opposed these plans but failed in their legal actions to prevent development. In a failing bid to improve judicial understanding, Stone (1974) proposed that trees, forests, oceans, and other natural objects in our environment could have legal standing. If natural objects have legal standing, they can be represented in the legal system and their interests protected: "We are widely regarded as having moral obligations toward infants, the insane, the terminally comatose—none of whom is reciprocally obligated to us. . . . In sum, there is no reason to accept the premise that because a tree or mountain cannot be a moral obligor, it cannot, *ipso facto*, be morally considerate in the thinking of those—we humans—who *are* moral obligors" (Stone 1993, 273).

In the sixteenth century, the courts did permit legal representation of nonhumans in trials against human accusers. For example, in 1587 the villagers of Saint-Julien in France took legal action to evict a colony of weevils from their vineyards. After a long trial in which the attorney for the defense played skillfully on many small points of law, the villagers decided to settle out of court before the magistrate rendered a verdict. The settlement permitted the weevils to lease nearby open land in exchange for moving from the vineyards. The villagers negotiated a right-of-way across the weevils' new home and the right to use the land as a refuge in case of war, but otherwise agreed to leave them in peace (Ferry 1995, ix–xvi). Ferry cites similar cases including one in which some leeches, who were present in the courtroom, were ordered to abandon the site they had temporarily invaded and were summarily executed when they refused.

Ferry argues that these cases occurred in a premodern or "prehumanistic" time in which humans saw themselves as rooted in a singular and whole creation of God. Liberal humanism, with its attendant human advantages of liberty and scientific investigation of the world, requires us to think of ourselves as distinct from the natural world: "Far from being bound exclusively to the value of *rootedness*, [civilization] finds its true elevation in this separation from the natural universe by which 'a world of the mind' is progressively forged" (Ferry 1995, 9). Only children of the Enlightenment would think of these trials as absurd.

This legal argument need only be based in interests; it is not necessary to grant nonhumans moral standing to be able to offer to protect their interests in law, but many authors do (Regan 1983; Singer 1985). Nonhumans may not be rational as commonly understood, but they have interests, perhaps life itself or even a continued habitual existence in a stable ecosystem, that should be taken into account in human projects.[6] When we see an animal bred and raised in a factory farm killed for human use can we really deny that "in some sense [the animal] is a party to the proceedings?" ("Also a Part of Creation") with some interests and rights.

Stone now believes that the legal rights argument is more practical than ethical or moral arguments, for "my first instinct—reinforced no doubt by being a lawyer—is to place principal emphasis on reform of law and social institutions, and steer clear of human spirit. Hard as social institutions are to change, they are a lot more malleable than human nature" (Stone 1993, 236). At the very least, he argues, humans would come to respect nonhumans more. However, he does not explain how a democratic state would change its legal institutions as he recommends without first changing humans' beliefs about the "value" of nonhumans.[7] Such substantial changes in legal systems must come after "the selection of an acceptable moral framework, [that] cannot itself be *derived* from any prior moral postulates. It is the answer to the question with which philosophy began—long before the contemporary preoccupation with valuing acts and (less often) actors: *How ought one to live*" (Stone 1983, 279–280)—a question of ethics, a problem for individuals, and one that remains unsolved.

RELATIONSHIP PROBLEMS

Bioregionalism argues that there is a synergistic relationship between human community and closeness to the natural environment. Ecofeminism locates the problem in the relationship between the genders.

## Bioregionalism

The social structures and institutions that separate humans physically and spiritually from nature (and from each other) prevent them from realizing their true selves. The increasing domination of human by human initially separates humans from harmony with nature and realization of human potential. The proposed solution is small communities that are directly connected to and reliant upon the local ecosystem. This project is partly cultural, as "society . . . attains its 'truth,' its self-actualization, in the form of richly articulated, mutualistic networks of people based on community, roundedness of personality, diversity of stimuli and activities, an increasing wealth of experience, and a variety of tasks." By integrating individuals into a community and the community into the local ecosystem, humans will recognize and participate in a wholeness, a "unity that finally gives order to the particularity of each of these phenomena . . . the relative completion of a phenomenon's potentiality" (Bookchin 1986, 53).

Thus, bioregionalism emphasizes decentralization; culture "predicated upon biological integrities and action in respectful accord; and a society which honors and abets the spiritual development of its members" (Dodge 1981, 114). Humans would be more fulfilled by integrating a just human community with the community of nature. Bioregionalism echoes many of the themes of communitarian writers: only just communities permit humans to realize their true selves. But it goes further, arguing that just communities are small communities anchored in the local ecosystem, not separated from it in large "parasitic" urban areas (Odum 1993) as is common in the modern industrialized world. In human groups properly rooted in the natural world—through regular interaction with it—relations between humans would be truly communal: small is just, as well as beautiful (Schumacher 1974; Sale 1980).

This vision of a sustainable, localized society runs counter to the reality of population movements from small towns to large cities and from rural to urban areas (*World Resources 1996–97*). Modern lifestyles, and the material dreams of the peoples of developing countries, require some trade interaction between communities.[8] The conveniences to which the industrialized world has become habituated would require technology for efficient microproduction to permit decentralized production and community independence. However, without complete equality in natural resources and technology, communities would remain dependent on each other or accept substantial difference in material wealth and well-being. Much of history is the tale of the dominance of materially weak communities by stronger ones.

A bioregionalist solution implies radical changes in social and political institutions. Decimation of trade connections and global markets threatens well-established global and local institutions. It conceives of a human nature that does not struggle for dominance and prestige, is social, mutually supportive, and closely identified with local ecosystems, very different from historical human nature, especially in the industrialized countries of the modern world.

## Ecofeminism

Ecofeminism argues that it is the defective relations between the genders that prevents an appropriate relationship between humans and their natural environment: the fault is in the man-centered nature of the dominant western culture. Active feminists at the 1992 Global Summit pointed out that the "crisis in development and the environmental crisis [are] inextricably connected with militarism, the nuclear threat, growing economic inequalities, violation of human rights and the persistent subordination of women" (Braidotti et al. 1994, 5). These problems emanate from a social system constructed in a male self-image. If human society better regarded what is "womanly," not only would it be more just to women but also to their kind: "the earth, the sea, the sky" (Daly 1987, 28). Women, it is argued, are by their biology or their social roles closer to nature.

For some ecofeminists, women's different character and concerns, values and behaviors, derive from their unique ability to give life and to care for a child, although caring for one's child need not automatically extend to caring for other nonrelated humans or nonhumans. Preventing an environmental crisis requires that caring female traits become more valued and a dominant foundation for human behavior. There is little agreement about these traits and there is little likelihood that they can be objectively identified. "We could only know what a representative sample of 'female' women would look like if we already had some idea of what female traits were, but then the traits would be announced *a priori*, as it were, rather than deduced through observation" (Dobson 1995, 189).[9] But if biology is so determinative of women, many potential personal projects would be incompatible with women's essence: "Man (and then woman . . .) is devoid of a specific function. It is impossible to read any type of destination into his makeup, to identify in his nature the sign of any sort of plan. A woman, it is true, can bear children: that, to speak Sartre's language is her *situation*. But to declare that she "is made to bear children" is to deny her liberty, to transform her situation into a *natural determination*, in short to 'animalize' her" (Ferry 1995, 5).

An alternative approach argues that women and men are socially determined in a male-dominated society. Women have hitherto been cast in the caring roles of elementary school teacher, nurse, and mother. Their movement into occupations such as businesswoman, doctor, and attorney would change their dominant qualities, the meaning of "woman" would change as their social role changed. Society defines what it is to be female. If women take on more male roles, humans may become *less* considerate of nature, suggesting that changes in concepts of "maleness" are more important. In the male world, knowledge is gained through scientific analysis, in which reason is elevated above feelings. Technology, the child of science, is used to dominate and control nature. Engineering Hall at the University of Wyoming bears these inscriptions: "The control of nature in the service of man" and "Strive on—the control of nature is won not given." In most modern societies, female roles—

caring roles—are devalued: both females and nature are "irrational, uncertain, hard to control, fuzzy" (Dobson 1995, 192).

Development is then seen as unsustainable because male society dominates nature as men dominate women. Defects in social relations and defects in relations between development and environment both emanate from the same biological male urge to dominate. The dualism of science is an essential precursor of dominance, for dominance and control are only possible over the "other" that is seen as separate from the self. This dualism is an essential component of the society constructed by and dominated by men. Thus, it is argued that dualism and dominance are male preferences, implying that men have an essential nature. The male perception of the female, and female nature, as different and separate, permits dominance of the female and of nature. Sustainable development requires that humans "see value not only in the natural world but in the characteristics which we as humans share with it, which have been allocated to the feminine and treated as culturally problematic" (Plumwood, quoted in Evans 1993, 184).

There is little agreement about the reason for the dominance of women by men (Dobson 1995, 193; DesJardins 1992, 255–256). If human societies dominate nature because of the dominance of one gender by another, a society *dominated* by women would also seek to dominate nature. The need to dominate must lie in male biology or male social roles, both of which have been too little investigated to conclude on the source of the desire to dominate. For ecofeminists, it is the "man-centered" nature of our culture that is to blame: "the deep ecology movement will not truly happen until men are brave enough to rediscover and to love the woman inside themselves" (Salleh, quoted by Ferry 1995, 117).[10] The changes in ideas about the nature of women and men or of their appropriate social roles necessary to sustain development will almost certainly be opposed by many cultural shibboleths and religious tenets, as well as social and political institutions. Ecofeminism does not explain how these obstacles will be overcome.


VALUING NATURE

Markets and modern democracies reflect a utilitarian ethic. Utilitarianism evaluates the expected consequences of any action to assess its 'rightness.' An action is moral when its consequences provide a net gain in happiness to the society as a whole. Motives are irrelevant and the distribution of this net gain in happiness is not considered "except that the more equal distribution is to be preferred to break ties" (Rawls 1971, 26). Thus, a moral act is one that promotes the happiness of the greatest number.[11] This can be criticized as a foundation for sustainable development. First, does "greatest" imply quantity or quality; and second, does the "greatest number" only count humans, and only those alive today?

Mill disagreed with Bentham, the founder of utilitarianism, over his understanding of the "greatest": "whereas for Bentham 'greatest' meant *most*, for Mill it meant *best*" (Miller 1993, 373). For Bentham all pleasures were equal; for Mill some pleasures were of higher quality than others (reading a book may be 'better' than watching television). He expected that those who had experienced the higher pleasures would continue to prefer them to lower-quality pleasures: "It is better to be a human being dissatisfied than a pig satisfied; better to be Socrates dissatisfied than a fool satisfied" (Mill, quoted in Miller 1993, 376).

Qualitative differences are subjective; the quantity of happiness— the "good"—can only be measured through individual choices as revealed in their actions. Whose good should be measured? Bentham did not exclude animals from the group of "sentient beings" whose happiness must be considered in measuring the rightness of actions (Bentham 1948, 311). For Mill (1957, 16) a pleasurable existence "might be . . . secured to all mankind, and not to them only, but, in so far as the nature of things admits, to the whole of sentient creation." However, the market values goods and services in accordance with their utility in creating subjective pleasure for humans. Because "there is no known human *use* for the [spotted] owl and because the owl does not contribute to human society in any obvious way" [emphasis in the original] it has no value (DesJardins 1992, 32). Such arguments ignore the aesthetic value of the spotted owl or its value as part of an ecosystem.[12]

As natural resources are consumed, they become of greater value and contribute more to the happiness of humankind by their exploitation. So, there is no objective and universal rule that would limit the exploitation of natural resources. Yet, as utility is measured by individuals, the more who find utility in the existence of unspoiled nature the greater the good from acting to conserve natural goods.

Alternatives to utilitarian ethics have sought to identify an ethic that separates nonhuman values from human uses. These efforts include Leopold's land ethic, biocentrism, inherent worth, and intrinsic valuation of nonhumans. I shall critique all four approaches together at the end of this section.

## The Land Ethic

The land ethic "reflects the existence of an ecological conscience, and this in turn reflects conviction of individual responsibility for the health of the land" (Leopold 1970, 258). Arguing that the land is the source and "fountain" of energy for nature, Leopold concludes that "an ethical obligation on the part of the private owner is the only visible remedy" (251) requiring curtailing rights of landowners with duties to the land-centered community.

Locke rejects his own initial argument for self-restraint—to leave as good and as much for others—because the market system releases individuals from the obligation to be self-restraining, requiring only that he or she not leave produce to be wasted (Locke 1980, 28). Leopold wants to limit the effect of economic property rights by attaching an obligation to conserve nature. Thus, property owners should have a responsibility to tend their land so as to maintain its ecological value, both for other humans and for nature itself.[13] Ethics must now include all aspects of the ecosystem ecology: "The land ethic simply enlarges the boundaries of the community to include soils, waters, plants, and animals, or collectively: the land" (Leopold 1970, 239). This will create a state of harmony between humans and the land they inhabit, that is not built on the concept of ownership of land but rather on a sense of "land as a community" to which humans belong (Leopold 1970, xviii–xix). In this ethic, "a thing is right when it tends to preserve the integrity, stability, and beauty of the biotic community. It is wrong otherwise." Human decisions should reflect "individual responsibility for the health of the land" and not merely be "economically expedient" (Leopold 1970, 258, 262, 279).[14]

## Biocentrism

Lovelock (1979) argues that the Earth is essentially a single living organism and that life has created for itself the conditions on Earth under which life can survive. The atmosphere, produced by the geosphere and the biosphere, "is an extension of a living system designed to maintain a chosen environment" (Lovelock 1979, 10). From this "Gaia" some environmental activists have created a biocentric worldview in which life is the central "good" of which humans are only one form. *Prima facie*, humans have no more value than any other form of life and no automatic right to use the rest of life to obtain our ends: "The Gaia hypothesis implies that the stable state of our planet includes man as a part of, or partner in, a very democratic entity" (Lovelock 1979, 145). The health of the Earth is not under threat from human activity. As Lovelock argues, "On a planetary scale, life is near immortal" (Dobson 1995, 45, quoting Lovelock). Nor does the Gaian hypothesis demand humanity's care of its environment: "It may be that the white-hot rash of our technology will in the end prove destructive and painful for our own species, but the evidence for accepting that industrial activities either at their present level or in the immediate future may endanger the life of Gaia as a whole, is very weak indeed" (Lovelock 1979, 108). The Gaia hypothesis does not prevent the substitution of species. The effect of human colonization of ecosystems may be to destroy the basis for human life without damaging Gaia. More recent versions of Gaia remove any teleological implication from the hypothesis but do not change its essence.

## Inherent Worth

Arguing from ecology that humans are part of a web of life, Taylor (1986) concludes that humans are only equal to, and not morally superior to, other organisms. Because every organism is a "teleological-center-of-life" with its own ends or purposes, of which both itself and we may be unaware, each organism has "inherent worth." The good of any living thing is the function it performs within the web of life: "each [organism] is a unique individual pursuing its own good in its own way" (Taylor 1986, 99–100). Life, at the level of individual organisms, must be respected.

In practice, humans as moral agents must not harm any organism, interfere with its freedom, or deceive or betray it, and must make restitution where harm occurs.[15] Human duties to conserve *individual* organisms make sustainable development a matter of individual choices, the ultimate decentralized decision making.[16]

## Intrinsic Valuation

Rolston (1988) argues that humans have no duty to protect individual organisms but that humans have no right to destroy species. It is more readily accepted that humans owe duties to sentient life forms: generally higher animals can be seen to feel pain.[17] But ants are "a ganglion on legs" not deserving of our moral consideration (Thomas 1975, 12). Supporters of animal rights often exclude lower life forms from moral consideration: "A life with no conscious experiences at all . . . is a complete blank; I would not in the least regret the shortening of this subjectively barren form of existence. . . . The life of a being that has no conscious experience is of no intrinsic value" (Singer, quoted in Rolston 1988, 94). However, if a single ant is not morally considerable, the collective of which it is an integral part, the ant *colony*, may be. However, Rolston (1988) argues that not only does each life form have a subjective value for itself but also an objective value in itself. Humans may perceive this value but do not create it: "Despite the language that humans are the *source* of value which they *locate* in the natural object, no value is really located there at all. . . . We humans carry the lamp that lights up value, although we require fuel that nature provides" (Rolston 1994, 15). Individuals may perceive these values differently, giving the impression that values in nature are not objective.

There is no agreement about the source of these noninstrumental values. It may be in a general reverence for life (Schweitzer 1946) or because a species is part of a whole and the stability or the location of that stability would be affected by its loss. Echoing Leopold and reflecting ecology, the value lies in speciating processes and ecosystems (Rolston 1988). Or perhaps the value lies in the natural processes from which the species was developed.[18] Organisms cannot have a disvalue because they annoy, harm, or obstruct us; their value lies in themselves, not in our uses of them. Intrinsic value occurs naturally and is an emergent property of natural entities, something that happens independent of the consciousness that observes it.

## Valuation Problems

While nonhumans may have a value beyond their human use, it seems probable that only humans value. As "values have no causal power to operate apart from value perceivers" (Nozick 1981, 437) humans must accept the responsibility of being the sole valuers able to act morally toward nature. The temptation to value in human terms is very great and the consequences of accepting that nonhumans have inherent or intrinsic values is enormous.

Extrapolating from a concept of a web of life, as do all attempts to create noninstrumental values for nonhumans, requires acceptance that what is natural is morally good. As Leopold (1970, 262) comments: "A thing is right when it tends to preserve the integrity, stability, and beauty of the biotic community. It is wrong when it tends otherwise." Morality becomes limited to upholding the accidental relations of extant ecosystems. Such value theories are more about the place of humanity within the biosphere than about any real intrinsic value of nature, and they avoid rather than solve the problem of environmental ethics (Taylor 1992, 115–119).[19]

Values are general principles of right and wrong that ought to guide actions. Valuing is part of what separates humans from nonhumans. It also requires conceptual separation of human from nonhuman. Liberal humanists argue that an essential aspect of humanity is freedom from biological determinism and an ability to be separate from the rest of nature. Humans are the arbiters of value (and responsible for all values) *because* they are separate from the rest of nature. Freedom from a biological human nature rooted in the biosphere allows humans to value but also leads to a view of "Mother Nature" as outside, remote, different, and nonhuman, part of the environment to be controlled as part of personal and communal projects. Thus, Ferry (1995) concludes that accepting intrinsic or inherent values in nonhumans would greatly reduce human liberty. Moreover, the acceptance of such values is an individual choice with extensive practical implications.

SPIRIT AND NATURE

Recognition of a humble place within a larger whole may also be cast as a matter of belief, as one might believe in God. Feeling at home within nature and within ourselves requires a deep belief in the connection with all life. If those deep feelings are religious, deep ecology has a religious component and "those people who have done the most to make societies aware of the destructive way in which we live in relation to natural settings have had such religious feelings" (Naess, quoted in Devall and Sessions 1985, 76). Saving one's soul requires preserving nature: "To understand natural systems is to begin an understanding of the self" (Dodge, quoted in Devall and Sessions 1985, 21).

## Deep Ecology

Deep Ecology is an "ecosophy" founded upon two connected "intuitions," of *self-realization* and *biocentric equality*. It is "a process of ever-deeper questioning of ourselves, the assumptions of the dominant worldview in our culture, and the meaning and truth of our reality . . . and goes beyond the so-called factual scientific level to the level of self and Earth wisdom" (Devall and Sessions 1985, 8, 65). Self-realization is only possible through identification with family, community, species, and thence with nonhumans. Biocentric equality demands that each organism pursue its "own individual forms of unfolding and self-realization within the larger Self-realization" (Devall and Sessions 1985, 67).[20]

Some activists have moved beyond cautious discussion of the ethical underpinnings of a green society to action intended to change behavior and beliefs. Although they hold ideas similar in many regards to deep ecology, these activists demand engagement in group action to inhibit human environmental encroachment.

## Ecotage

Nonviolent sabotage of ecologically destructive human activities, is practiced by activist groups such as *Earth First!* From an initial ploy to suggest the potential danger of a breach in the Boulder Dam, they have moved to various acts to inhibit commercial activity from land development to mining and forestry (Manes 1990). Because modern life exacerbates separation from the natural environment and is spiritually hollow, they believe that the time has come "to make the choice between the natural and cultural world" (Manes 1990, 139–40, 240).

Although deep ecology and ecotage activists use similar mantras, the former advocates a personal search and the latter a form of communal, political action. The difference is between one conversion at a time or an effort to convert the institutions that prevent individuals from recognizing their plight. Ecotage is intended as a practical implementation of deep ecology. However, there is a contradiction between individual self-realization and collective action undertaken to change the minds of others. Is it not hypocritical to proselytize an individualist religion?

CHANGING MINDS

Ecologism theories have at least two important policy-related defects in addition to the technical problems alluded to in the foregoing discussion. First, these theories purport to describe a common goal (a common state of consciousness necessary for the desired social order) with little or no discussion of the means necessary to achieve that goal. Second, political activism (an obvious means by which to make wholesale changes in social values) is opposed to the individualism implicit or explicit in each theory. Thus, they offer no foundation for a mass political movement.

## Ends and Means

Ecologism theories commonly describe an ideal state of human consciousness by which humans will better relate to and conserve nonhumans. They describe a goal or end without explaining the means necessary to that end.

Ecologism's goal is to change the world by changing the ideas that humans hold of their place and purpose within nature.[21] This unintentionally mirrors the thinking of Antonio Gramsci, an Italian communist leader who proposed a nonviolent alternative to social revolution. Gramsci argued that the power of the dominant class came not only through material structures but also through ideology. Members of the dominated class have a "conception of the world" that is not their own but that of the dominant class. Changing material political and economic structures alone requires state coercion to achieve radical social change. True social revolution is the result of a social movement in which the dominated class develops its own ideology before acquiring government power. In this way the consent of the people will support and bolster radical change. State coercion will be unnecessary; the revolution will be the will of the people (Forgacs 1988, 190–220; Hoffman 1984; Pellicani 1981).

Similarly, the ethics narrative asserts that development cannot be sustained through the political and social institutions developed for a world of assumed abundance. Humans would have to accept radically new ideas—beliefs and values—about their relations to the nonhuman world. However, an ecological worldview will only drive policy if enough individuals and decision makers learn to understand their existence and purpose in new ways.

Although not often specifically mentioned, the business of changing minds is the purpose of education.[22] With enough of the right sort of education, individual preference sets should converge, permitting cooperation in the making and following of policy on sustainable development. Education can come in many guises, but to sustain development (a long-term project) it would have to touch nearly everyone on the planet. Global civil society would become imbued with beliefs and values comparable to those in the theories reviewed in this chapter. Two primary sources are formal public education systems and nongovernmental public interest groups.

Because formal (school) education imbues cultural values and because knowledge of sustainable development is politically constructed, education to sustain development would be a political activity. Thus, if formal education is expected to change beliefs and values, a community would have to decide to change the beliefs and values of its members through education *before* they receive that education. A communal decision to influence beliefs and values is unlikely to precede a change in the beliefs and values of a majority of the community. A crisis might in the short run achieve a change in beliefs and values, perhaps as a result of a misconception of the problem, as in stratospheric ozone depletion between 1974 and 1976 (see Dotto and Schiff 1978). Otherwise, action to sustain development by changing beliefs and values through formal education could come from decisions of an autonomous state—Ophuls and Boyan's (1992) philosopher-kings—or by serendipity.

A large number of ENGOs work hard to change the environmental beliefs and values of the people (McCormick 1989). Much of peoples' increased concern for the environment seen in all industrialized and many developing countries can be credited to the success of ENGO education efforts. However, there is a big difference between increasing public sensitivity to single environmental issues and a mass ethical conversion. Other nongovernmental organizations whose main purpose is not the dissemination of environmental ideas (for example, churches and labor organizations) may find the values and beliefs they espouse conflict with those that the ethics policy narrative argues are required for sustainable development.[23] Finally, there is no assurance that an uncontrolled exchange of ideas through various media (the World Wide Web, e-mail listserves, etc.) will change beliefs and values appropriately or rapidly enough to sustain development.

## Individualism and Political Movements

Some deep ecologists believe that "we can change the conventional political process by using it for deeper purposes" (Devall and Sessions 1985, 29). Other analysts argue that the nature of ecologism prevents it from offering a coherent political program that can be pursued in modern democratic political processes (Goodin 1992; Dobson 1995). None of the green analytical approaches reviewed here offers a theoretical underpinning to a political movement. None is a political ideology that could act through collectivities (such as political parties) within a democratic political system. Each can change individual minds and social and political institutions from the bottom up. None can offer a guide for coordinated political action.

Because ecologism is more concerned with "the organization of whole societies rather than of mere political parties" (Goodin 1992, 147), it lacks a unifying political ideology. Green political parties have had to modify their political platforms to be elected, becoming much less radical as a result (Sarkar 1990), but group political activity is anathema to the radical, individualist ideas that will sustain development.[24] There is an inconsistency between the green theory of agency and the means by which a green theory of value, a "unified moral vision," may be pursued. Thus, Goodin (1992, 171) concludes that the belief in decentralized social organization must be sacrificed in order to organize the mass political movement: "There is simply no place for preciousness and keeping one's green credentials clean when the fate of the earth hangs in the balance." However, this would be to abandon a central principle of the green theories of ecologism, that it is important that people voluntarily accept green ideas. The green theories are connected by a common belief that only a change in human consciousness can rectify the damaged relations between humans and nonhumans. Learning, accepting new ideas and applying them in your life, can only be voluntary. If, as economics and rational choice assume, self-interest is the sole foundation for human action, then behavior can be changed without changing minds. Learning in such theories is only Pavlovian: how to achieve the unchanging desire under changing conditions. If the principle of voluntary learning is abandoned, it would not matter how people get the right ideas as long as they behave in accordance with them. Such an argument could be used to support almost any form of coercion to save the Earth. Who then will save humanity?

The conservatism of those who have benefited from 'brown' growth (most of the industrialized world and controlling elites in many LDCs) means that "nothing beyond reform is possible" and "environmentalism and ecologism diverge rather than converge" (Dobson 1995, 209–210). The environmentalism Paehlke (1989) describes is effective precisely because it is incremental and intelligible to the common voter in a way that ecofeminism, biocentrism, or deep ecology is not.

Environmentalism has been effective because it provides a foundation for mass political action through current political institutions. Environmentalism is "an extension of liberalism in its claim that the basic human rights established by liberalism belong also to future human generations and to other species." It is "a political movement that seeks to impose upon the physical sciences and engineering restraints based on the findings and judgments of the social and life sciences" (Paehlke 1989, 191–192, 117). It has "clear links with all the classical ideologies. But to be effective it must also stand alone; it must become an autonomous political ideology in its own right" (193) and its supporters "must find means of relating their ideas to the issues of principle concern to those actively involved in the political world" (244). The effectiveness of ENGOs in placing environmental issues on the political agenda (especially in the industrialized countries) and the electoral success of green parties in Europe shows that environmentalism is—already a decade after Paehlke's exhortation—a mainstream political ideology changing the policies of political institutions, not changing those institutions.[25]

Environmentalist opposition to specific issues, from dumping of used oil drilling platforms to French nuclear testing, to whaling, is well publicized. Yet, the sum of these media moments probably does not create a green consciousness for a single voter. Environmentalists fight political battles over single issues, while a more radical war over the ideas that underpin modern societies is ignored. Environmentalism may support a more political movement but it will not lead to ecologism's ethical goals. An airplane is not built by adding carriages to a train; they are fundamentally different modes of transportation. To stay true to its theoretical roots, ecologism cannot embrace mass political action.

CONCLUSION

Unlike the other two narratives, the ethics narrative encompasses diverse theories from more than one discipline. Nevertheless, there are commonalities between these theories that should be considered for sustainable development policy. First, an assumption common to all ecologism theories is that the world is constructed in human minds: that ideas are important. The meaning commonly attributed to reality reflects social values and beliefs evolved over time to enable effective and productive social interaction within defined human groups. Currently held values and beliefs do not sufficiently conserve natural goods to the level necessary for sustainable development; the world they construct (and which humans act upon) is unsustainable. Each ecologism theory offers an ideal ethic of values and behaviors adapted to a world with natural limits.

Second, all theories expect that 'human nature' can be changed, that it is more malleable than Hobbes and economic and rational choice theorists assume. Human nature is the collection of essential human motivators.[26] These motivators are not solely a characteristic of the physical body; they also reflect the mind. Ideas of right and wrong influence motivation and desires. As ideas evolve, so does human nature. Cannibalism recycles waste human bodies to sustain the living and has, in the past, been practiced by many human groups. Yet, it is now widely considered to be completely "unnatural" (not in the nature of humans) to eat humans.

Third, although these theories do not admit as much, their silence on means suggests that ecologism theorists understand that intentionally changing ideas (values and beliefs) on a large scale is very difficult. Ideas, values, and beliefs evolve slowly over time, rooted in culture and protected by social institutions. Even if ideas can be changed, it is not clear that they can be changed precisely and fast enough for sustainable development. Despite Orwell's predictions for 1984, forced reconstruction of ideas through propaganda is rarely, if ever, successful and would be anathema to the green understanding of learning.

Finally, the focus on idealist ideational structures suggests that, in some form, education must be central to any effort to radically change ideas about the appropriate relations between human and nonhuman. A change in ideas is learning, often achieved by education. However, education policy faces a bootstrap problem. How can policy change before ideas change? Thus, the proposed reliance by Ophuls, Daly, and others on coercive, but enlightened, governments.

There is no easy path to the nirvana of ecologism. Indeed, green theorists have notably failed to illuminate *any* path. However, it is clear that policy for sustainable development must consider the inside of the human mind as well as institutional change.

# 8

## POLICY PRINCIPLES FOR SUSTAINABLE DEVELOPMENT

Sustainable development is a Holy Grail that does not exist. It is a legend, a myth. But like every myth, though untrue, it serves a purpose. As this book has shown, sustainable development cannot be objectively defined, cannot be known. Sustainable development cannot be defined as a certain state of society that will result by adopting specific, definable policies or individual behaviors. It cannot be a social goal. You might think that if you don't know where you are going, any road will get you there. To travel without a destination is to travel aimlessly. However, sustainable development is the journey—not the destination—and some principles for policy choices along the road are necessary. The purpose of this chapter is to generate those policy principles for sustainable development and suggest some early applications that may be adapted to the needs and conditions of individual communities.

A rational model of policymaking defines goals from among contending utilities or interests and assesses the costs and benefits of a small range of alternatives. Policymakers select the alternative with the highest net benefit as measured in terms of the chosen goal.[1] Another approach, suggested by the equity narrative, would be to explicitly consider questions of the distribution of costs and benefits throughout domestic and international societies. Finally, if humans only thought differently about their place in the world, policy choices could be self-evident and universally supported. None of these approaches comprehends the problem of sustainable development.

This chapter shows that policy for sustainable development can best be understood by modeling human systems as complex systems. This view of sustainable development legitimizes discarding modern concepts of truth, universality, and reason-driven progress. "Postmodern" ideas that accept contingency, decentralization, and subjectivity (which emphasize process over goals, means instead of ends) seem most appropriate. But as postmodernism in the social sciences is poorly defined and remains much disputed (Best and Kellner 1997), it does not provide a sure foundation for policy. However, theories of complex adaptive systems, considered a postmodern scientific method based in the life sciences, do suggest a theoretical and conceptual model of sustainable development as a continuous process for which policy principles may be defined but for which there is no specific goal. If human society, faced with the problem of sustainable development among the uncertainty of ecological limits, is modeled as a complex adaptive system, its self-organizing adaptive capacity (that which in living systems seems to be the measure of life) is an appropriate criterion for optimization. Sustainable development policy becomes the problem of continually optimizing "social adaptive capacity" as ecological systems, and human knowledge and ideas about them, change. Policy must be flexible, creative, and rapidly adaptable to changes in knowledge and human values and beliefs.

Because sustainable development is a concept that includes everything, it is a commonplace to recommend that it can only be studied by breaking down barriers between disciplines. Yet, to reflect the comprehensiveness of the issue requires more radical theorizing. The first section of this chapter discusses the deficiencies of goal-oriented narratives. The second section proposes complex adaptive systems as a metaphor of human societies and derives general principles for sustainable development policy from the characteristics of such systems. These principles add up to optimization of social adaptive capacity. Differences in the state of development, technological capacity, ecosystem constraints, and so on in each locality make it impossible to propose policies appropriate for every community. However, this chapter's third section offers some initial directions for sustainable development policy.

PROCESS AND GOALS

Policy is usually thought of as the setting of social goals. For example, "policy states an intent to achieve certain goals and objectives through a conscious choice of means and usually within some specified period" (Kraft and Vig 1990). Such definitions of policy reflect the essence of modernism (the philosophic and aesthetic theoretical foundation of modern societies): that goals can be known, selected, and with appropriate means, reached. Modern societies are teleological, consciously selecting goals and a preferred future state: "We have a goal; we have a problem, which is a discrepancy between the goal and reality; and we seek a solution to erase the discrepancy" (Stone 1988, 8). Modernism assumes that humans are rational, that the world can be known through the application of ordered reason (i.e., science) and expressed as universal truths that apply everywhere at all times. Thus, progress comes from accumulating scientific knowledge ("truth") and leads toward perfection—the termination of all that is "bad" in society. Reality is conceived as ahistorical and unaffected by culture and social relations, and what is true is also good and right.

The three policy narratives are stories that describe the policy means for reaching the goal of sustainable development. In modern societies, dominant élites foster narratives, stories that societies tell themselves about the rightness of their philosophical and political ideas and beliefs, to maintain order and social cohesion. Each of the three policy narratives describes an ordering of society for sustainable development. Each policy narrative has a unique premise (a value preference) or premises, but each is defective in its internal logic. None can define sustainable development broadly enough in policy-relevant terms to fully capture the concept. As the analysis in the preceding chapters has shown, each proposes an incomplete, impractical, or ineffective path to sustainable development. Each narrative is a rhetorical combination of facts and values that embodies certain ideas about social structures and the nature of the relationship between humans and nonhumans.

Some policy theorists argue that where "the values and interests of opposing camps are so fundamentally divided that no middle ground for compromise exists between them . . . the best alternative is to forgo searching for consensus and common ground in favor of a metanarrative that turns this polarization into another story altogether" (Roe 1994, 4). The sustainable development metanarrative would be " 'told' by the comparison" as the story of the discourse between the dominant narratives of sustainable development analyzed in the preceding chapters.

Any narrative is an effort at the unification of fragmented society through a hegemonic rhetoric, a set of values and beliefs that if generally accepted would permit communal action. It is the pursuit of a goal, a state of society by means of a rhetorical device. The purpose of a metanarrative is to transcend barriers between policy advocacy groups thrown up by uncertain data and differences in values and perceptions. It is a political exercise designed to reinterpret reality to allow policy action and end gridlock. A metanarrative serves the needs of those who demand action on sustainable development policy. But it would remain a narrative with exclusive premises and its own (now interdisciplinary) logic. A discursive metanarrative might seek some trade-off between efficiency, equity, and ethics, some rule of exchange between these values in the pursuit of the goal of sustainable development. However, limited knowledge of the human impacts on the natural systems that support development render any narrative, including a discursive metanarrative, too confining to make policy useful. A metanarrative would constrain and direct thinking toward a goal, a more inclusive goal than described by any of the three current narratives, but a goal that cannot be sustainable development.

The concept of sustainable development presents a problem for modern theorists because it cannot be objectively defined (by science) and subjective understandings vary widely. Interpretation of phenomena depends on one's standpoint (Diesing 1982).[2] Values and beliefs (whether or not ethical, i.e., embedded in an internally consistent set of values and beliefs)—what I call "ideas"—taint or color perception much as tinted sunglasses change the color of reality: perception is through and by means of values. For the capitalist, sustainable development is a problem of production efficiency and technological innovation; for the environmentalist, it requires a change in consciousness about environment; and for the honest LDC policy maker, it is an insufficiency of material goods and democratic political institutions. As commonly understood, sustainable development can be interpreted to support any agenda or objective. In that sense sustainable development seems to be the ultimate "postmodern" issue. Modern beliefs in progress, social improvement, human domination, and teleological history through rationality have lead to the production expansion that has greatly increased material wealth but challenged ecological limits. Sustainability is a question raised by modern life. Unfortunately, *post*modernism proposes no conclusive answer to this question.

The several schools of postmodernist thought are linked by a common opposition to the post-Enlightenment modern project. Postmodern theories reject "truth, certainty, universality, essence, and system and . . . grand historical narratives of liberation and revolution." They "abandon mechanical and deterministic schemes in favor of new principles of chaos, contingency, spontaneity, and organism . . . [and] often embrace a radical scepticism, relativism, and nihilism" (Best and Kellner 1997, 6, 19). Where modern theory assumes an underlying order in natural and social events, a universal truth that could be discerned through reason and empiricism, postmodernism does not. All is contingent and uncertain, local and subjective. There can be no universal sustainable development policy, no true path of sustainability to be discovered.

Rather than seeking a universal solution to fragmentation, difference, and contingency in social life, postmodernism embraces them.

Postmodern politics is "associated with locally based micropolitics that challenge a broad array of discourses and institutionalized forms of power" (Best and Kellner 1991, 5). As a panacea for this extreme subjectivity and fragmentation, postmodernism proposes greatly increased political participation (as in the equity narrative) or a new sensibility (as in the ethics narrative). While increasing the participation of subjectively interested groups in policymaking may solve the problem of minority exclusion, it does not ensure effective collective action and may inhibit it. Sustainable development policy is too important to be left to the vagaries of unguided pluralistic decision making among myriad subjectivities; and any new sensibility may be long in coming. Postmodern politics is concerned with increasing the volume and variety of voices, not with solving a collective problem such as sustainable development. However, as the next section shows, generalized principles for sustainable development policy derive from a form of postmodern science.

### COMPLEX ADAPTIVE SYSTEMS AND POLICY PRINCIPLES

Modern orthodoxy founded on a mechanistic ontology (or "social metaphor") cannot grasp the problem and will lead sustainable development policy astray. Visualizing human society as a machine leads theorists and policymakers to expect that social goals can be selected and targets achieved. The effects of policies, they believe, can be known in advance, allowing policies to be tailored to the goals desired. The belief that outcomes can be known makes the process of policymaking particularly unpleasant—no more tasteful than making sausages. As each participant believes she knows the probable outcomes of each proposed policy and as each has learned to be self-interested, she fights for the policy that is least damaging to her interests.

Because of the imprecision and complexity of the problem and the incomplete understanding of ecosystems and human systems and their interactions, a mechanical model is particularly unsuited as a guide to sustainable development policy. At the heart of the efficiency and equity narratives is a mechanistic model: human society is a machine in which outcomes can be predicted from actions. In the ethics narrative, the structure and operation of the ethical society is not described in any detail; only biocentrism lightly sketches the ethical society. All ecologism theories expect that changing ideas will change institutions and behaviors predictably, and an equilibrium between human wants and ecosystem needs will be achieved. Thus, the ethics narrative is also founded on a mechanistic social metaphor, though less explicitly so.

Both human society and its natural environment are complex adaptive systems in the sense that "a great many independent agents are interacting with each other in a great many ways" (Waldrop 1992, 11). These systems (and their component systems) are also adaptive—they can actively respond to changes in their environment—and may exhibit characteristics of "spontaneous self-organization" of constituent units into the patterns that distinguish the system.[3] Concepts borrowed from biology and other life sciences seem to best explain complex adaptive systems. Such systems are like organisms; indeed, the characteristics of complex adaptive systems seem to be a metaphor of life itself.

Recognizing the reliance of humanity on natural systems, it is appropriate to model human society as an open complex adaptive system such that "there is basically no duality between man and nature. . . . We are part of nature ourselves. We're in the middle of it" (Arthur, quoted in Waldrop 1992, 331–334). Once duality is eliminated, it is not meaningful to talk about optimization. There is no object to optimize and there are no parameters for optimizing the whole. Thus, it is wise "to keep as many options open as possible. You go for viability, something that's workable, rather than what's 'optimal'. . . . What you're trying to do is maximize robustness, or survivability, in the face of an ill-defined future. And that, in turn, puts a premium on becoming aware of nonlinear relationships and causal pathways as best we can. You observe the world very, very carefully, and you don't expect circumstances to last."

The principal characteristics of complex (that is, living) systems outline the policy principles for maximizing survivability and, thus, for sustainable development. First, complex adaptive systems have emergent properties. Second, they adapt to changes in their environment. Third, they are dynamically balanced between chaos and order, like life. Fourth, they draw energy from their surroundings to maintain their internal order. Fifth, complex adaptive systems are indeterminate and unpredictable.

## Emergent Properties

In mechanical systems, the operation of the system can be calculated from the characteristics of its constituent parts and the system structure or the principle that orders and connects the parts. An internal combustion engine would be a good example. Spark plugs, cylinders, fuel injection, and pistons interact in an ordered way to produce power. In contrast, complex adaptive systems have emergent properties: the whole is more than the sum of its parts. Systems' behaviors are produced by the interaction of their constituent units, and by the emergent system properties created by those interactions. In living things the emergent property is life. This means that system behaviors cannot be predicted from the aggregate of interactions among its parts. The behavior of the system will emerge spontaneously from the operation of the system.

As complex adaptive systems, human communities have emergent properties that distinguish them from each other and from random collections of individuals.[4] In a real sense the community is more than the sum of its members. It is something made by their interaction: the community has a life of its own. Human communities are not merely aggregations of individuals who seek similar desires in the same way. They are not only the sum of individuals, or of their relations and the institutions that order those relations. Communities have a life of their own that is more than the individuals, institutions and material properties, values and beliefs, shared language, and culture. Communities are living organisms; they evolve and change in ways not predictable from the behaviors of individuals or from changes in institutions or ideas. Viewed as a complex adaptive system, each community has needs distinct from the needs and wants of individual members. Sustainable development policy should address those communal needs as well as the needs of individual members.

Because sustainable development is probably only possible through collective action, maintaining the health of communities becomes especially important. The health of the system, a function of its emergent behavior within its environment, also affects the health of its parts. An animal out of its natural environment is poorly adapted and likely to suffer illness and death, which affects its internal organs. Similarly, while individuals eventually will be affected by unsustainable practices, the problem and the solution reside in human communities.[5]

## Adaptation

The essential characteristics of a complex adaptive system emerge from the self-organization of the interactions among its agents. Because the environment for each agent is all the other agents in the system as well as the system's environment, agents can be said to "co-evolve." For example, cells interact cooperatively to form the physical features of an animal and to give it life. Agents interact to form "meta-agents," systems that are themselves agents of another system (Holland 1995, 6). Cells are agents within an animal that is an agent in an ecosystem.

Each agent within a complex adaptive system behaves in accordance with an internal model of its environment constructed from regularities in information it receives. A predator finds its prey using an internal model of their usual location and behavior. Even components of the human immune system appear to use simple "tacit" internal models to identify dangerous invaders (Holland 1995, 33). Agents change their internal models and, thus, their behavior as experience accumulates. This is a localized form of adaptation.

Such learning may be insufficient for survival. The system's health depends upon its ability to adapt to environmental change. Large changes in the environment may demand structural changes in the complex adaptive system. Structural change results from changes in the interactions among agents within the system. Evolution is the selection by the environment of those patterns of agent interactions that optimize the system's health. Because the environment of individual human communities consists of other human communities and of natural communities or ecosystems, they can only sustain themselves by adaptation to *both* aspects of their environment just as individuals adapt to the behavior of other humans and to their physical environment.

Policy is the initial means by which communities adapt to their human and natural environments. Policies are guided by internal models of those environments. These models change with the development of scientific knowledge and new ideas. Successful policies may be copied by other communities. In the long run, humanity may only survive by encouraging experimentation in social forms (mutations) among constituent communities and communicating the successful experiments for other communities to adopt. Unlike natural systems, through the interplay of ideas human systems may use changes in internal models (policies) to create mutations, new social forms. For example, Lenin and his successors used policy to drag Russia from medieval feudalism to a 'communist' modernity. More successfully, various policies in the early nineteenth century changed Britain from an insular mercantilist state to a dominant free trading, capitalist, industrial state. Policies that change institutions or the ideas and beliefs of a majority of the polity, either directly or by modifying behavior, can lead to new social forms.

Adaptation may have to anticipate ecological limits. Exceeding an ecological limit changes the system; this is a one-way trip. Once the global climate has changed as a result of anthropogenic emissions, only adaptation is possible. Ideas, and the institutions that transmit and embody them, must evolve before conclusive evidence that an ecological limit has been transgressed. Thus, adaptation should be precautionary and not wait for scientific certainty.

There are three ways in which human systems can adapt to environmental changes. First, most commonly, humans make themselves comfortable in the natural environment through tools and technology.

Second, primitive human systems adapt their institutions and practices to their environment. Nomadic cultures of the steppes differed from agricultural communities in the Nile River valley; each ordered its social life in accordance with its natural environment. Because technology has allowed modern societies to dominate and manage their natural environment, their institutions do not have to take account of environmental changes. However, as Daly proposed (see chapter 3), institutional change could be used to reduce the consumption of natural goods. Third, as proposed by the ethics narrative, changes in ideas affect relations between humans and their natural environment. If ideas (that are the connection between the long-term adaptation of humanity and local behaviors) change, so do perceptions of the need to change human institutions. Recognition of the proximity of environmental limits could encourage multiple modes of adaptation in human systems.

The modern conception of separation between humanity and its environment is directly coupled with the rise of modern exploitation of natural goods. The acceptance of technology as a panacea for environmental ills, of unfettered markets for organizing economic activity, and of individualism and self-interest as foundations for social life directly or indirectly explain much of the rapid growth in natural goods consumption. Such ideas order relations between humans, and between humans and nonhumans.

## Order and Chaos

Complex (living) systems exist "at the edge of chaos" (Waldrop 1992, 302–303), balancing sufficient disorder to permit adaptation with enough self-organization to exist as a system. Life is not wholly random and chaotic as the theory of evolution suggests (Kauffman 1995). It is self-organizing into patterns that repeat themselves. We see order from self-organization in crystals of copper sulphate that always grow the same way, in the symmetrical form of snowflakes, and oil droplets forming spheres in water. Similarly, human communities should be institutionally and ideationally flexible while retaining the emergent properties that make them communities and more than collections of individuals. Adaptive change should not change the community *qua* community. As recommended by the equity narrative, participation in the decisions that affect their lives ("consent of the governed") will strengthen communities and enhance collective action. The concept of self-organization—a spontaneous (but in human systems conscious and considered) ordering of units into a system—also suggests the importance of voluntary participation rather than externally imposed organization. Consent of the governed can be most effectively achieved by applying a principle of subsidiarity: that decisions should be made at the lowest practical level of organization. Localizing policy would also help to educate the largest number of individuals about the importance and complexity of sustainable development.

## Dissipative Structures

Living organisms (and complex adaptive systems) are dissipative structures drawing energy from their environment to "maintain themselves in a stable form far from equilibrium" (Prigogine and Stengers 1984). Life processes maintain themselves by converting low-entropy resources to high-entropy waste. Thus, like other living systems, humans and human communities "are islands of order in a sea of disorder, maintaining and even increasing their order at the expense of greater disorder in their environment. . . . Order 'floats in disorder' " (Capra 1996, 189–90). As open systems interacting with their environment, living systems may change their environment and, sensitive to environmental changes, they must be dynamically adaptive to the environmental changes they have themselves created—that is, they have a "dialectical" relationship with their environment (Levins and Lewontin 1985). Human society inevitably draws in energy (in material form as natural sources and sinks). However, the degree of environmental disorder thus created should be minimized, if only to reduce the need for future social adaptation through policy. Sustainable development policy should reduce the rate of consumption of natural goods. This could be achieved in three ways. First, the size and rate of growth of human population could be reduced. Second, ecological efficiency could be enhanced with an ecological techno-economic paradigm. Third, consumer wants and demands and, thus, consumption could be directly reduced.

Population control would obviously be helpful, but coercive institutions might reduce the social cohesion necessary for effective sustainable development policy. Population measures based in education and empowerment of women have been effective (World Resources 1994–95). However, cultural taboos on birth control need to be taken into account. Each of the policy narratives examined here avoids explicit restraint on population growth as the central means to sustain development, although for some analysts this is critical (Ehrlich and Ehrlich 1968 and 1991; Hardin 1968; Daly 1993). The three sustainable development narratives effectively assume that population will increase and that the rate of increase is culturally determined. Population growth is not an important issue in the developed world where per capita consumption is greatest, and in most developing countries rigorous population control is no longer an acceptable policy topic. China's legal restraints on fertility are designed for practical purposes rather than long-term sustainability. Indeed, China could face a severe labor crisis (potentially a problem for economic development) as its single child cohorts (baby bust?) come of working age and their larger parents' generations age and retire. As the LDCs industrialize, education programs aimed at reducing fertility become increasingly important.

The efficiency narrative recommends that technological innovation be directed at increasing ecological efficiency and basic research at creating an ecological techno-economic paradigm. The inevitable draw of energy from natural systems by humanity demands no less. In developed countries, community direction of the allocation of funding for basic research may be necessary. Developing countries could select and adapt items from the technological shelf. Because these are produced in developed countries for their economic needs (reducing labor cost in a low capital cost environment), developing countries should carefully consider their individual national economic and ecological needs. This may require technological assistance from developed countries and international mechanisms to transfer the most eco-efficient technologies while preserving patent laws.

Though transmitted through production technology, consumption of natural goods depends on demand for goods and services in the satisfaction of human wants and needs. Without a change in ideas about the value of nonhumans, it is difficult to imagine voluntary, radical reductions in consumer demand. As suggested in chapter 3, consumer demand could be marginally reduced with various incentives acting through market prices, particularly in the form of taxes.

## Flexibility

Because of their complexity, living systems' future states cannot be predicted beyond the very near term. With sufficient information and knowledge of cause-effects relations, future states of mechanical systems are predictable. Because it is a closed system, the future position of a tricycle can be predicted with sufficient information about energy input, friction, wind resistance, and so on.[6] Living systems can only be modeled mathematically by nonlinear equations, most of which have no solution or have multiple solutions. Intrasystem feedbacks make even simple nonlinear systems with singular solutions very sensitive to infinitesimal calculation errors or roundings of decimals or to small changes in initial conditions. If future states of human society cannot be predicted, the effects of policy are unpredictable. Even the most scientifically "perfect" policy may have significant unintentional effects on natural ecosystems or human systems. *Policy should remain flexible, able to adapt rapidly to new information and new ideas.*

Sustainable development will be inhibited by inflexible institutions designed for other purposes. For example, institutions designed for elite maintenance, economic growth, or colonial expansion will probably prevent sustainable development. Institutions that reduce social adaptive capacity should be removed. Institutions naturally evolve and change: cannibalism and suttee are dying out, friendly societies became labor unions, governments set the rules for financial reporting to protect capital markets. For sustainable development, institutions should change through policy in response to new information and ideas rather than through social evolution.

Policymaking is rank with uncertainty even in much visited issue areas (such as welfare, poverty, and foreign policy): outcomes rarely accord with expectations and unintended consequences may be more significant than the planned effect. In reality most participants in policymaking rarely can predict their interests. If they do not *know* the outcomes of specific policies (and they can never *know* outcomes unless this policy has previously been tested under these circumstances), they cannot know which policies accord with their interests, even if they are clear about which outcomes they desire. Beliefs about outcomes generate policy squabbles; an appropriate humility should promote a collective search for the policy in each case that best enhances survivability of the community.

## Social Adaptive Capacity

The complex adaptive systems model leads to five principles of sustainable development policy that add up to a need to build social adaptive capacity. These principles extend and expand the admonitions of the three narratives to increase ecological efficiency, to increase equity (and therefore participation in collective behavior and community cohesion), and to change environmental ethics or ideas about relations with nonhumans.

First, the community (the organism that individuals constitute) has needs, separate from those of the constituent individuals, that should be directly addressed. While individual communities should apply these principles within their (human and natural) environments, they should not ignore the needs of higher levels of collective organization (state, region, etc. and *homo sapiens*). Communities cannot solve their individual problems by passing pollution down river or by dumping into a global common pool resource.

Second, the objective should be to adapt by any means possible, including deliberate modification of institutions and ideas, to new information about the effects of human activities on ecosystems and changes in the values that influence perception of the environment. As proposed by the ethics narrative, in the long run ideas should change to optimize adaptability. Policy should anticipate environmental changes; thus, the precautionary principle should guide decision makers.

Third, policy should balance adaptation with maintaining community. As the equity narrative argues, social cohesion (aided by participation in policymaking) should enhance collective action. Subsidiarity would enhance political participation and social learning.

Fourth, in agreement with the efficiency narrative, ecological efficiency should be optimized as suggested in chapter 4 and through appropriate use of market mechanisms (see chapter 3).

Fifth, because policy outcomes are unpredictable, sustainable development policies should remain flexible. Policies will not achieve expected outcomes and unanticipated effects will occur. Flexibility in policies, institutions, and ideas is imperative. Experimentation and change are essential.

Collectively these principles add up to "robustness" or enhanced social adaptive capacity. This is the *capacity of a human community to adapt to its (human and natural) environment through ideational and institutional changes while maintaining social cohesion and collective action.* It is a measure of the survivability of each individual human community and, collectively, of the human species. It includes not only changes in technology but also changes in the fundamental organization of communal life, including policies, institutions, and the ideas that underlie and are embedded in institutions. Social adaptive capacity will be greater the wider the range of policies, social behaviors, and institutions that may be changed and the faster their response to changing facts or values. However, the community must maintain its cohesion for a collective response to be possible and effective.

Human communities cannot exist without order. Because increased participation of individuals in the decisions that affect their lives tends to encourage individuals to participate in collective action, order should be voluntary (designed by the ordered) rather than imposed. Symbols and structures from tradition, culture, and stable institutions provide continued collective identification through which communities voluntarily adhere. However, community cohesion should be balanced with an ability to change institutions and practices. This balancing act has so far eluded most societies. The traditions and institutions that provide social cohesion can too easily lead to social sclerosis (e.g., Olson 1981). An excess of change can lead to fragmentation of social allegiances and loss of the cohesion that makes a society or a community out of an assortment of individuals.

Sustainable development as the pursuit of social adaptive capacity reflects a re-conception of human society and its constituent communities as complex adaptive systems; this is a change in ontology. It is *not* a metanarrative: these principles of sustainable development policy do not constitute a new story of society. They are *principles* because they do not advocate specific actions in the pursuit of selected values, and they are principles of the policy *process* through which collectivities can sustain themselves in an uncertain future. Increasing wealth in the stock market is, as Will Rogers said, a matter of buying low and selling high. That is a principle, one that does not define actions but is a rule for action in the pursuit of wealth. These principles of sustainable development policy do not define specific actions or specify outcomes. They are rules for survival in the face of the unknown.

Sustainable development is, then, a state of mind, a way of perceiving the world, not a materially definable goal. However, it is a state of mind that is less esoteric—and probably more acceptable to the large numbers of people who must participate in its policymaking—than the ideas demanded by ecologism as summarized in chapter 7.

This approach is not specifically postmodern. However, it does borrow some ideas from postmodernism, such as contingency and the rejection of truth claims. Nor does it reject science; some knowledge is possible from reductionist methodologies and all knowledge would be useful. Pursuit of these principles of sustainable development policy should avoid the policy narratives' presumption of values (and make values the subject of political discourse) and should focus attention on sustainable development as a central but indefinable concern of all people and all communities everywhere.

DECISION MAKING ON PRINCIPLE

Indeterminacy, the central feature of sustainable development policy, is reflected in the policy principles described above. Sustainable development is a process of continuous adaptation of policy to humans' changing perceptions about the world around them. These policy principles should be applied in all decisions at whatever level of organization, whether they are decisions about new development in an American suburb, logging in Indonesia, or fishing on the high seas. Choosing policy by applying principles rather than by allowing the competition of interests demands a new model of decision making.

Policy and decision making processes are commonly modeled as a compromise of utility functions among interested individuals and groups. Each participant assigns utilities to policy alternatives in accordance with their individual interests. This model shows how the needs of the collective (society or community) can easily be overlooked in the search for a policy that satisifies the interests of the largest number of participants. Although satisfying participants may ensure their continued participation in collective life, ignoring the needs of the collective in favor of individual needs reduces opportunities for joint gains.[7] As this model of decision making becomes widely accepted as true, self-regarding behavior in collective decision making becomes more firmly entrenched. However, not all decision making does ignore collective needs, as the research of Ostrom (1999; Ostrom et al. 1994) and her colleagues has shown.

A model of decision making that emphasizes values, or in this case principles, rather than interests and personal utilities, would increase the importance of communal needs in decision making and would connect every collective decision with sustainable development. It would encourage qualitative construction of desired objectives from an intense scrutiny of values. As with utilities, value functions, value trade-offs, and multiple values analyses may be constructed. These differ from the normal utility functions in being explicitly the result of detailed analysis of values. Usually values are wholly subjective: "For each of the fundamental objectives, the answer to the question 'Why is it important?' is simply 'It is important' " (Keeney 1992, 78). However, if the values in decision processes reflect the principles derived above, value-focused decision making would become the heart of the sustainable development process. As discussed above, removing policymaker hubris that outcomes can be predicted with any useful probability should make value-focused decision making more attractive.

Within each decision context, the principles of sustainable development policy would define the values to be pursued. For each progressively lower-level objective, the focus would be on outcomes that satisfy those principles within the specific decision context. Policies would be chosen not from among a limited range of alternatives in response to a problem, but to further application of the principles of sustainable development: "Rather than a need, [value-focused thinking] is a desire to do better, to strive towards the best possible consequence in terms of our values, that leads to the identification of decision opportunities" (Keeney 1992, 47). For sustainable development, the best that can be achieved is to optimize social adaptive capacity—or "survivability"—everywhere, at all times.

The next section suggests some initial policies in the direction of survivability that should emerge from decision making driven by sustainable development principles (rather than interests).

Some books about sustainable development include a long litany of specific policies that will make the goal achievable.[8] The technical capabilities, human and physical capital resources, low population growth and highly managed ecosystems in developed countries give them policy opportunities not available to LDCs. The United States with its continental size and low population density faces different challenges than the island of Great Britain, despite some similarities between the two cultures. However, based on the principles of sustainable development policy, there are some initial policy directions that should be applicable, with some adaptation, nearly everywhere.

## Community

Both locally and globally, community should be strengthened. To build local collective action, direct participation in decision making should be encouraged and rewarded. Often there are effective local institutions for collective management of common pool resources. Where these do not exist they should be encouraged. Decentralization of decision making to the lowest practical level would seem appropriate; centralization of decision making is likely to make decisions less locally appropriate and less flexible.

The international system would be a good place to start: to coordinate local decision making with global communal needs demands reform of the international system (as well as some national decision making systems). Interdependence reduces the ability of all states to pursue their outcome preferences. Environmental interdependence through global political and economic structures threatens the ability of any country to protect its natural environment and maintain its development. Without change in international political and economic structures there is a low probability that these structures will permit less developed countries to develop as rapidly as necessary while conserving their own and global natural environments. Because absence of government makes change in the international system more tenuous, global policies that encourage a sense of community between countries and influence their identity formation—how they see themselves and choose their outcome preferences— are essential to globally sustained development. Enhancing the participation and the influence of LDCs in global policymaking should encourage their adoption of the proposed principles of domestic policymaking and improve coordination of global sustainable development activities. If they remain flexible and adaptable, international institutions (including intergovernmental organizations) should aid the process. Contrary to the exhortations of the Brundtland Commission, they do not assure success. Piecemeal treatment of individual international environmental issues will not suffice. Substantial increases in bilateral economic, technological, and educational aid from developed to developing countries should greatly enhance both LDCs' interest in cooperating on global sustainable development and their individual social adaptive capacities.

There seems to be an inherent and insoluble conflict between local community decision making and modern capitalism. Globalization of production has been driven by many factors, including innovation in production and control processes which allow for smaller production units.[9] Further technological innovation may increase dispersion of the production system into self-sustaining smaller units, completing the cycle begun by the initial organization of work into factories. Or it may increase the globalizing connection between local production units. The choice is social rather than wholly technical. Complete decentralization of production and authority, though not an immediate prospect, should help sustain development.

## Increasing Ecological Efficiency

The allocative efficiency of markets can be used to aid in sustaining development. However, free markets are not a panacea; they are a means, not an end. The focus of policy should be the macro relations of the market to social purposes and ecosystem needs rather than an ideological attachment to free markets. Political institutions can implement policies that direct the market toward eco-efficiency.

For the market to aid in sustaining development, natural goods must be appropriately priced. As suggested in chapter 3, taxation is one tool for increasing the cost of consumption of natural goods. It also avoids direct, politically imposed restrictions on rights (of property and propagation). Taxation could be increased on ecological "bads" with an eventual goal of replacing taxation on income from productive activity.[10] Price signals will encourage both consumers and producers to favor more eco-efficient products and processes. A natural goods use tax assessed on each stage of production (as value-added tax is now applied) would encourage eco-efficiency in each step of the production chain. This would require improved measures of eco-efficiency, and ecological financial reporting and green auditing.[11] Markets and market actors (such as firms) are eminently adaptable. Governments should use this strength to solve social priorities such as sustainability of the system (rather than of a particular ordering of the system).

Consumer demand can be reduced or modified, and redirected through a consumption tax assessed on the amount of income not saved (thus, on that portion consumed). Allowances for certain types of consumption—or more properly for a base amount of consumption—should minimize the most regressive effects of such a tax. However, once again the effect would be to increase the cost of an activity that is ecologically bad without preventing that activity.

The difficulty of changing systems of taxation cannot be overestimated. Many groups will prefer to keep the present systems under which they have become wealthy and powerful.[12] However, broadening political participation as suggested by the equity policy narrative should aid this transition.

Many issues of principle and practice can be raised against these and other suggested changes in price signals through taxation. Price signals will be most effective in redirecting investment if they are known in advance. Taxes could be implemented progressively in accordance with a published schedule (perhaps over ten or twenty years). Investment in alternative transportation fuels would be encouraged through a policy that raised the price of liquid hydrocarbons a prescribed amount annually over an extended period. The cost to the end user of fossil fuels could be increased over time by setting the tax as the difference between the market and an increasing target price. Although this might make government budgeting more complex, it would simplify planned investment in alternative energy forms.

Policy should also point technological innovation at the problem of eco-efficiency. Taxation on natural goods use should encourage demand for eco-efficient production. However, firms have historically relied upon government-funded basic research to create the scientific knowledge from which market demand selects. Firms are better adapted to incremental application of new knowledge in response to market pressures. To enable an ecological techno-economic paradigm, governments should approach the management of basic scientific research for eco-efficient production as they have the production of knowledge for technological warfare. Technology-forcing initiatives such as early development of the Internet, contracts for digital control of manufacturing (Noble 1984), and space research have driven the information age and the growth in communications technology. Placing a large number of small bets on basic research in a number of areas such as materials (e.g., superconductors), energy (e.g., alternative transport fuels), and bioengineering should stimulate eco-efficient technologies.

Again LDCs are faced with different problems. If they have or can develop the necessary governmental capacity, they should select among the innovations on the technological shelf for those that improve eco-efficiency *and* aid development. Because enhancing material wealth and well-being is a part of sustainable development (especially in the poorer developing countries), the most eco-efficient but capital-intensive production might initially be less effective for sustainable development in an LDC than a more labor intensive but less ecologically efficient technology.

## Information

A quick surf of the World Wide Web will convince all but the most skeptical that there is a great deal of useful data about sustainable development policies and practices that have been tested and found to be effective. However, these data need to be collected and corrolated in a database available to all so that experiences are shared, learning enhanced, and effective institutional forms identified. Similar centralized sources of information about local initiatives within a country should be constructed by each state. A successful program or policy in southern Kenya should be more useful as a guide for practice in Kenya and Tanzania than in Texas. However, to enhance global learning, all these data collections should be accessible by all. A few dollars for international assistance to LDCs for construction of these databases could be highly effective.

## Education and Ideas

To optimize social adaptive capacity, humans eventually will have to accept a less privileged place within the global ecosystem. Dissemination of ideas such as those summarized in chapter 7 (the ethics narrative) would help to change consciousness of nonhumans needs and thence human behaviors. This should also lead to a greater consideration of the "other," thus generally improving community.[13] A civil society with ethical concerns about relations with nonhumans and other humans is more likely to curb its consumption of natural goods through individual, decentralized decisions and collective policy.

Education about new ideas and approaches should be encouraged. Ethics and ecology could be a more important part of formal education. Public discourse over ideas should be focused in local groups trained in basic principles of ecology, in value-focused thinking, and in the principles of sustainable development. Active participation by ENGOs and other special interest groups should be encouraged as long as they pursue these principles and recognize the fallibility of policymaking. Single-issue environmental politics may motivate local action, but it does not build the necessary consciousness of the more general problem of sustainable development. Serial saviors of whales, forests, and Wyoming toads distract attention from the wholeness and complexity of the

because it is renewable only over geological time scales, so its natural limits are the quantities found in the Earth's crust. Agricultural goods are the result of a "process," as are the oceanic uptake of atmospheric carbon dioxide and the "digestion" of the wastes from human processes.

5. Diesing (1982) argues that such subjectivity is inevitable in social science because the scientist is part of the experiment. Policy may be socially contentious even if the problem can be objectively identified. But without an objective definition of the problem that may be available in certain narrow issues (perhaps, the connection between smoking and health costs), any issue becomes colored by the subjectivities of social science.

6. Without theories, general statements about reality or about possible futures would be impossible.

7. The term *eco-efficiency* was popularized by MacNeill et al. (1991).

8. In the eighteenth century the distinction between (noble) savage and civilized man was commonplace. "Civilization" in this sense meant social order, hierarchy, mechanization, monotheistic religion, and so on. Civilization is much less easily definable today because of the absence of a contrapuntal savagery. Indeed, the improved killing efficiency of modern weapons, the 100 million people killed in wars in the twentieth century, and the extreme quality-of-life differences between rich and poor, within and between countries and communities, suggests that modern "developed" societies are very savage and seem to lack much civility.

9. Increasing social equity is also expected to conserve the environment. People may be driven by poverty to overuse resources, and traditional farming practices may exhaust the soil and yet fail to feed a rapidly growing population. More developed societies use more eco-efficient agricultural production techniques.

CHAPTER 2. SCIENTIFIC KNOWLEDGE AND UNCERTAINTY

1. Examples include Ophuls and Boyan (1992); World Commission (1987); Miller (1992); Schneider (1989); Porter and Brown (1991); Brown (1991 and 1992b); Ehrlich and Ehrlich (1991 and 1992).

2. See, for example, Arnold (1987); Simon and Kahn (1984); Ray and Guzzo (1992 and 1994); Bailey (1995). In global climate change alone the rebutters include Balling (1992); and Michaels (1992).

3. "Proven reserves" are estimates of known, economically viable reserves; these estimates increase or decrease in response to changes in prices or technologies even if no new ore bodies are found. Technological innovations may increase the quantity of the resources that can be obtained from known ore bodies. While it may be technically possible to mine asteroids, it may be legally and politically difficult, and will probably not be economic for many years ("How to Mine a Flying Mountain").

4. The range for the estimated global sustainable catch is from 68.82 to 96.23 million metric tons (MMT)—a range (equal to about 40 percent of the minimum estimate) that indicates significant uncertainty in these estimates (*World Resources 1994–95*).

5. A rational belief (as about what actions will sustain development) is one that is held while "not believing any statement less credible than some incompatible alternative" and "believing a statement only if the expected utility . . . of doing so is greater than that of not believing it" (Nozick 1993, 64, 106).

6. Other outcomes in between these extremes are also possible. For example, mitigation efforts may turn out to be insufficient to sustain development, but at least catastrophe would have been delayed.

## CHAPTER 3. THE EFFICIENCY NARRATIVE

1. Neoclassical (or "orthodox") economics is the "normal science" (Kuhn 1970) of the discipline. This is the collection of theories and methods accepted by the majority of economists and enshrined in economics textbooks; it is taught to undergraduates, is prominent in policy proposals, and has now, like pop psychology, in part passed into the language of the nonspecialist. Environmental economics is an adaptation of neoclassical assumptions and methods to solve temporally and geographically local (and primarily interpersonal) environmental problems.

2. In the tradition of Hayek (1994) and Friedman (1962), personal liberty in a pluralist society is a primary goal of modern economics. Thus, the market is a "political-moral institution for the maintenance of individual freedom" (Rothschild 1993, 48). Although not every economist would be so explicit (many would perhaps focus on the tools and the methodology rather than some moral purpose), this is a central value of orthodox economics and, thus, a premise of the efficiency narrative.

3. The freedom advocated by economists such as Friedman and Hayek is often considered a negative freedom: freedom from restraints on property rights. This libertarian freedom contrasts with the positive freedom of liberalism discussed in chapter 5.

4. Galbraith (1976) argued that advertising influenced consumer preferences. Although his analysis has been roundly criticized by many economists, his argument is intuitively reasonable. It is not clear how much advertising influences consumer choices, but that certainly is its purpose, and the weight of advertising in support of product differentiation encourages priority of market-produced goods over goods not provided by the market.

5. Neoclassical economics assumes that consumers are only self-regarding, ordering their want preferences in accordance with internal desires,

ignorant of the wants and actions of others, except through market price indicators. However, fashion and other forms of social pressure are evidently important factors in consumption decisions.

6. In modern industrial economies, poverty is relative rather than absolute (Fields 1980). For example, the poverty level in the United States for a family of four is defined as one-half of the median income for a family of two adults and two children.

7. Contributors to ENGOs exchange their financial support for a promise to provide certain services, such as protection of specific natural species or environmental education and political lobbying. Contributors may not receive those services directly; they expect the ENGO to provide such services publicly.

8. Public or collective goods are those goods that are nonexcludable and indivisible; all have access to them, and your enjoyment of the good does not reduce mine. The classic example is national security. Whether or not you pay your taxes, the government cannot exclude you from protection from invasion. If you are protected, so are all other residents of the country. Other examples include law and order and, in the United States, the interstate road system.

9. Concentrations of production or consumption power also cause markets to fail. Although concentrations of market power influence economic choices that affect the consumption of natural goods, they are not important to the present discussion. Of more importance is the ability of highly conservative industrial interests, more concentrated and with narrower and more cohesive goals than consumers, to influence government environmental policies.

10. A distinction can be made between a "common pool resource," which focuses on the natural characteristics of the resource, and a "commons," which assumes certain social arrangements and human behaviors. A commons is a resource to which, because of prevailing social structures, a number of persons are granted rights of open access and use. Hardin (1968) seems to have derived the concept of the commons from the grazing land appropriated for communal use by villages in medieval England to which all households were permitted access and from which strangers were excluded. Hardin argues that rational action by self-interested users will eventually lead to the tragic destruction of the commons. This ignores the possibility that social institutions may be created that will prevent overuse (Ostrom et al. 1994; Ostrom 1990).

11. Common pool resources (such as ocean fisheries outside national 200-mile limits, the stratospheric ozone layer, the global atmosphere, and public forests such as the Amazon jungle), though open to all, are limited and invite overexploitation. In practice, it is often difficult to discriminate between public goods and common pool resources. Generally, economists think of clean air, clean water, and biological diversity to be public goods that are underprovided (Tietenberg 1994, 39). A greener image is conjured up by arguing that air, water, and the global gene pool are commons that inevitably will be overexploited and destroyed by self-interested, rational actors (Hardin 1968; Olson 1965).

12. Assume that the carrying capacity (based on the rate of growth of grass) of the Common in my hometown is eighty sheep, and there are twenty families in the village. Each family may graze their sheep on the Common. It is rational for a self-interested utility maximizer to put a fifth sheep on the Common when there already are four grazing from each family. That family will gain one sheep at the cost of one-eightieth of the common resource. Eventually all will lose when the grass fails to grow as a result of overgrazing. Meanwhile those families who grazed the most sheep will have gained the most in the short run from their overuse of the common pool resource.

13. Even if the government maintains ownership but permits private use, leases or other contractual use rights must give sufficient private control over a long enough time period for the lessee to want to manage the resource for dynamic efficiency.

14. Scarcity rent is the excess economic return resulting from the relative scarcity of the resources. Producers are assumed to be price takers unable to influence prices in a perfectly competitive market. Economic costs of production do not include any intrinsic value of the resource. Scarcity rent partially corrects this omission.

15. Except for politically motivated production restraints, as by the OPEC cartel, technical factors make supply inflexible in the short run. Optimizing the total take from a reservoir requires matching the rate of extraction with the reservoir's structure. Increasing the pump rate to extract oil earlier may damage oil paths in the reservoir, reducing total production. Also when stripper wells' (low output) production costs exceed market prices, they often remain pumping because they would require a costly workover to return to production once shut down.

16. As the discount rate increases, the shadow of the future shrinks. At a discount rate of 10 percent, a benefit of $1 million to be received 10 years from now is the same as receiving $385,542 today; receiving the same benefit 100 years from now is the same as $72.57 today, discounted at the same rate of interest.

17. This essential deficiency has not prevented economists from extrapolating environmental strategies long into the future (Solow 1986; Cline 1992; Nordhaus 1990).

18. For example, if a factory produces airborne pollution that causes acid rain on a downwind lake, killing the fish population, those people who fish in that lake, or who earn their living from the fishing (boat rentals, tackle sellers, fishermen, etc.) incur an economic loss and suffer other disutility (aesthetic) as a result of the factory's production. The factory is leaving others to bear the cost either of environmental damage or of rectifying that damage.

19. It is both difficult to measure the services provided by natural sinks and the sustainable rate of their depletion and more complex to allocate sinks (than sources) to individual owners. For example, direct privatization of the carbon

sink capacity of the oceans or of the stratospheric ozone layer is improbable; indirect privatization through quotas is possible. Private landfills properly maintained as a closed system are an example of privatized sinks.

20. This would not apply to intangible utility losses such as loss of existence values (Tietenberg, 1994, 46–48).

21. There has been speculation that global warming may lead to a nonlinear climate response. For example, see Schneider (1989) and Houghton (1994).

22. In 1991, the United States and India, among others, believed that their adaptation costs would probably be lower than mitigation costs (Interviews with representatives of the U.S. Department of Energy and the Indian Ministry of Foreign Affairs). For many less developed countries, such as Bangladesh and most small island states, the reverse was true. See Harrison (1994).

23. To assess the social cost of pollution over the Grand Canyon, both those who visit the Grand Canyon (who have a use value) and those who gain utility from knowing that it is there (who have an existence value) would be asked to assign a value to the natural good of clean air and high visibility over this natural wonder. This "value" can be used to determine the socially appropriate use cost or rate of tax to be applied to Arizona power generators emitting the pollution that causes the haze over the Canyon.

24. In economics, rationality is generally understood as transitive preferences in the pursuit of self-interest. In a transitive preference ordering, you prefer A to B and B to C and A to C. You will not impulsively choose C in preference to A.

25. Neoclassical economics also has been criticized as being "excessively staticized" because "all the determining relations are assumed to describe functional dependencies that occur together at a timeless instant" (Vickers 1994, 8–12).

26. Simplification and selection are necessary for any theoretical representation of reality. Theories are "rays of light, which illuminate a part of the target, leaving the rest in darkness. . . . Since it is a changing world that we are studying, a theory which illumines the right things at one time may illumine the wrong things at another. This may happen because of changes in the world . . . or because of changes in ourselves (the things in which we are interested may have changed)" (Hicks, quoted in Goodwin 1995).

27. The Carter administration's alternate energy program funded by the Windfall Profits Tax on fossil fuel exploration and development activities is an example of weak sustainability, because it tied investment in alternative and renewable resources to the rate of exploitation of nonrenewable resources.

28. Consumer freedom is an aspect of human freedom, and an important one if consumers use goods and services to construct themselves.

29. Many economists support extensive government intervention in markets to reduce pressure on ecosystems. See Krugman 1998.

CHAPTER 4. ORGANIZING A TECHNOLOGICAL FIX

1. A recent trend in scholarly writing about sustainable development builds on critiques of the need for the market to encourage an ever-expanding range of human wants and means to satisfy them. This genre grows out of Marxian critiques (O'Connor 1994) but also has echoes in Keynesian economics. See Galbraith (1976 and 1978) and others such as Schmookler (1993).

2. In 1998, the U.S. Department of Energy's Pacific Northwest National Laboratory identified the ten most important impending technological innovations that will lead to a cleaner environment and improved consumer services. These included: agrogenetics, smart water treatment, renewable energy systems, microtechnology, paperless display and communication systems, molecular design, bioprocessing by microorganisms, real-time environmental sensors, green companies and total product recycling, and lightweight cars (EarthVision News Reports, 4/20/98 published on the World Wide Web at http://www.earthvision.net/).

3. When Daly and Townsend (1993) suggest that the steady-state economy is most likely to sustain development, they expect innovation to be targeted solely at reducing throughput without increasing consumer want satisfaction. The efficiency narrative assumes that technological innovation can avoid resorting to such social engineering.

4. The respected weekly newspaper *The Economist* frequently publishes examples of the failure of government directed R&D. See, for example, "When the State Picks Winners"; "How Does Your Economy Grow?"; "The Machinery of Growth"; "Laboratory Truths from Abroad"; "Of Strategies, Subsidies and Spillovers." Studies from the 1970s and 1980s questioned government capabilities in this area. See Rothwell and Zegveld (1985).

5. For example, Nehru and the Congress Party of India fervently believed in the social benefits of science. Despite extensive poverty in India at independence, this socialist party accepted that a primary task of government was the establishment of a series of scientific research institutes and universities (Morehouse 1971; Nayar 1983).

6. Innovation can be distinguished from invention. Invention is "simply the bright idea for such a new product, process, or system" (Freeman 1992, 59) that may have no commercial potential, or its eventual application to satisfying human wants may be very different from that envisaged by the inventor.

7. In the United States, progressive tightening during the late 1970s and early 1980s of CAFE (corporate average fuel economy) standards raised the mean fleet efficiency of U.S. automobiles. It encouraged changes in engine design (for example, the move to direct fuel injection and computer control) and the increased use of lightweight materials (Saturn's plastic doors). Because of Americans' love of their cars, and now their sport utility vehicles, this only reduced the rate of growth in transportation consumption of fossil fuels. See MacKenzie (1990).

8. The uses of learning by doing and learning by using in LDCs are discussed in Aaron Segal, *Learning by Doing: Science and Technology in the Developing World* (Boulder: Westview Press, 1987).

9. In the natural paradigm natural products such as wood and water were used directly as goods (wooden eating utensils) or for production (water driven mills).

10. There is also extensive research at the level of the firm of the factors that support innovation. See, for example, Martin 1994; Tidd et al. 1997; and Rumelt et al. 1994.

11. According to Goldstein (1988), long wave variations in international economic activity may be explained by capitalist investment, technological innovation, crises in capitalism, or war. Schumpeter suggests that technological innovations cause such waves. Rothwell and Zegveld (1985) show that economic cycles are driven by eruptions of innovations, especially new technology systems (see also Goldstein 1988, 31–32, 50–55). Other scholars argue that technological innovation is an adaptive response to war as a threat to the survival of the state (Goldstein 1988, 32–39). In contrast to Romer (1986), other explanations diminish the importance of innovations in economic cycles.

12. Although firms are able to influence and sometimes radically change their market environment (Nelson 1995), the relationship between actor and environment is not usually considered dialectical as proposed by Levins and Lewontin (1985).

13. In principle, technology does not so much replace human labor as displace it. During this century the industrial countries have seen a movement of the majority of labor from the land to manufacturing, then to services, and recently to information production, manipulation, storage, and assessment.

14. Weinberg (1986) argues persuasively that technology is often used to substitute for social engineering (radical changes in social structure or living habits). Although Winner (1986) argues that technologies are not "autonomous" but a consequence of social choices, in practice, political action can only slow down or reduce the impact of the technological changes that the economy selects. There are few examples of a society consciously refusing to use a major technological innovation. Famous examples are the moveable type printing press in China (that because of the Chinese use of pictograms was impractical); Chinese use of gunpowder only for purposes other than warfare; and guns in Japan. The Chinese and Japanese societies were at the relevant times feudal and highly regulated.

15. Peer review of articles submitted to journals and of research proposals are the major means of ensuring 'quality' in the process. However, these methods also encourage marginal modification or elaboration of knowledge (what is known) rather than creation of new ideas about reality.

16. Faster transportation was sought before the motor car or aircraft were invented. However, these specific technologies were not demanded. Once early versions of automobiles had been created, some individuals, such as Henry Ford, could see the potential for production of large numbers of cars to satisfy the general desire for faster, cheaper, and more dependable transportation.

17. Empirical research (especially in the history of technology) into the progenitors of individual innovations often illustrates the complexity of connections to scientific knowledge and earlier technologies. Important new technologies are sometimes as much the result of fortune as of planning. However, individual technologies may be pursued to fill a specified need, as was often the case in Cold War military and space technology. See Noble (1984) and Wilson et al. (1980).

18. While it is possible that in the industrialized and "rich" countries the annual rate of increase in material consumption may decrease, the "poorer" developing economies will continue to attempt to emulate current rich world consumption practices. Education of consumers might reduce the rate of want accretion in both rich and poor countries, but probably through different mechanisms, with poorer countries using more government intervention in markets than governments in rich countries.

19. Moore and Miller (1994) argue that developing environmental technology is economically beneficial. Research into the core scientific knowledge upon which an ecological techno-economic paradigm could be constructed is likely to be even more so. Discovery of eco-efficient technologies also reduces the demand for natural resources, reducing the economic cost of competition over resources (see their comments at page 133 fn19). R&D into such technologies should reduce defense equipment costs; it should be in the interests of ARPA (the "Defense" in its title has now been eliminated) to direct research toward reducing resource consumption. Since World War II, the demands of technological warfare have diverged from consumer market demand, reducing the spin-off of consumer from military technologies (Thurow 1986). Direct conversion of military to civilian aircraft is no longer possible; though the C-3/Dakota of the 1940s and the Boeing 707 were developed from the B-47 and B-52 bombers, B-2 bombers are unlikely candidates for conversion to civilian uses. However, facilitating and financing basic research into ecologically efficient technologies should provide civilian benefits either in reduced consumption of natural goods or economic benefits, or both.

## CHAPTER 5. CONSIDERING EQUITY

1. Sources for these definitions of politics include Easton, Schmitt, and Arendt as quoted in Moon (1993).

2. For most political theorists, terms such as equity, justice, and fairness are almost synonymous; here it is not necessary to distinguish between

them. Political theory is largely concerned with defining what is an equitable distribution of the benefits of collective life. According to Rawls (1971), for example, an equitable distribution means that every member benefits in some measure from participation in that life. However, other theorists such as Nozick (1974) offer a property rights argument that justifies greater inequality in the distribution of collective benefits than Rawls would accept. Recently much political science has been more concerned with positively describing and explaining political activity than assessing the equity of the resulting distribution of benefits (Crotty 1993).

3. "But justice is the bond of men in states, and the administration of justice, which is the determination of what is just, is the principle of order in political society" (Aristotle 1885, 5).

4. Coleman (1994) also places the blame for environmental problems with government failures. As the founder of the green party in North Carolina, he reflects many of the views of the green parties of the United States and Europe. However, as chapter 7 illustrates, green politics encompasses an important paradox, suggesting potential problems with the solutions that green parties advocate. Also see Paehlke (1989) and Brown (1992a).

5. Even if all members of a group perceive an individual benefit from communal action, there remain substantial incentives to free-riding: they will "*not* voluntarily make any sacrifices to help their group attain its political (public or collective) objectives" (Olson 1965, 126). By offering positive and negative incentives, labor unions overcome the tendency among workers to free-ride on the industrial action of others.

6. Although feminism has influenced some political theorists, I shall discuss it (in its ecofeminist guise) in chapter 7. Feminism is more important for its critique of the dominant values and methods of political science, offering as a political project alternate values and ethical concerns. For sustainable development, ecofeminism is a part of the "green critique" of the dominant humanistic approach.

7. Galbraith (1976) is the economist commonly associated with arguments about the effects of unequal market power. As process technologies progress, raw labor is less demanded and capital becomes more important to profit-seeking firms. This process may be enhanced by globalization of markets (Kuttner 1996, 72–105).

8. The recent popularity of libertarian ideas in many developed countries may derive from a fear of a "slippery slope"—from equality of opportunity promised by liberalism to equality of outcomes (Schwarzenbach 1988; Kymlicka 1990, 109–118, 149–152).

9. Where Marxism uses social ownership of property to prevent unequal power relations, liberalism emphasizes the value of an equitable distribution of property to enhance individual liberty. Liberalism addresses the problem

of "each according to his needs" directly where Marxism uses a more indirect approach. Other Marxian critiques of private ownership of productive resources (capitalism), such as of exploitation and alienation, also add little to contemporary liberalism (Kymlicka 1990, 171–193).

10. Smith completed the sixth edition of *Theory of Moral Sentiments* (*TMS*) shortly before his death, more than a decade after his *Wealth of Nations* (*WN*) was first published. The error of ascribing to *TMS* the study of the altruistic side of human nature and to *WN* the study of the egoistic side is common. See Raphael and Macfie (1976, 20–25) and footnote 1 on page 10 of Smith's text. *WN* does not oppose *TMS*; it extends it in more detail in the economic realm alone.

11. Under certain circumstances, spontaneous local institutional arrangements have been effective at regulating use of common-pool resources. See descriptions in Ostrom (1990); Ostrom et al. (1994). Ostrom (1994) argues that such arrangements are possible even if individuals are assumed to be exclusively self-regarding, a stricter test of cooperation than discursive politics would apply.

12. Postmodernists generally argue that scientific information does not exist separately from the political structures and power relations within society (Best and Kellner 1997; Foucault 1980; Litfin 1994). Ophuls and Boyan's (1992) philosopher-kings may be untainted by politics but would not be able to identify an objectively optimal policy because of this insufficiency of scientific knowledge.

13. In Jackson, Wyoming, regular meetings were organized under the rubric, "Common Ground." Another example of local cooperation between local environmental conservationists and the logging industry in the American West is recorded in "First, Ask the Locals" in *The Economist*. Also see Page (1997) on solutions to New Mexico grassland problems and Pooley (1997) on saving a Colorado mountain valley from excessive development. These examples of communal action to preserve a commons and those offered by Ostrom (1990) all occurred in small communities. It is more difficult to envisage 260 million people in a geographically diverse country acting communally, or the more than 180 countries in the international system.

CHAPTER 6. SUSTAINABILITY IN THE INTERNATIONAL SYSTEM

1. In historical materialist theory, exploitation of the peripheral states by core states is a structural imperative. A less extreme position probably acceptable to most international political economics theorists is that there are extreme inequalities in the international system that inhibit the development of the poorer states. See Wallerstein (1979); Palma (1978); Gilpin (1987).

2. Structural change has usually been the result of armed conflict (Gilpin 1981). I assume that large-scale war is not a means to sustainable development.

3. Most discussion of international relations is positivist, seeking to explain the behavior of states around current issues within the present international system (Smith et al. 1996). Renewed interest in theories of ethical behavior

within the international system and the green theories examined in chapter 7 offer some hope for an international relations theory and practice worthy of humanity. Historically, international ethics was limited to issues such as 'just' war. More recently (Nardin and Mapel 1992; Frost 1996; Mapel 1990), theorists have discussed how ethics can be brought into all aspects of international relations. In this respect it serves a comparable role to political theory as a foil to positivist political science.

     4. Geographically defined and sovereign participants in the international system are "countries." Generally, "state" is reserved for the entity within the country that selects the country's goals and represents it in international negotiations. This may be thought of as the government, though because of the various influences on official decision makers, the state usually is more extensive than formal government institutions. The interests of the government and the political elite in foreign affairs may not coincide with the interests of the electorate they represent. In authoritarian regimes this divergence is usually much more evident than in democracies (Ferguson and Mansbach 1988, 111–142; Krasner 1978).

     5. The international system is anarchic because it lacks a ruling entity; anarchy is not the absence of rules, merely the absence of a governing entity with a legitimate monopoly on authority and the use of force. As Peter Kropotkin is alleged to have said, "Anarchy is not the absence of rules, only the absence of rulers."

     6. In the Trail Smelter Case settled in 1941, a lead smelter caused pollution across the Canadian-U.S. border. The emitter was held liable. Subsequent treaties encode comparable duties of care on their signatory states. See Blegan (1988). Customary law now reflects a broad duty of care toward the environment of another country.

     7. Although some critics argue that neither problem necessarily requires cooperation between states on a global scale, a majority of observers and practitioners accept that coordination of domestic policies to reduce emissions of ODSs and GHGs will be necessary to mitigate these problems. Roe (1994) argues that climate change could be combated by local action, for example to increase fuel efficiency. The "no-regrets" approach proposed by the United States until 1993 as a solution to climate change sought sufficient other benefits, including economic gain and diplomatic freedom of maneuver to justify policies that would reduce U.S. carbon equivalent emissions (United States 1991). The Vienna Convention on Ozone Depleting Substances with its protocol and amendments is a putative solution to the problem of stratospheric ozone depletion (Benedick 1991). Kyoto Protocol to the United Nations Framework Convention on Climate Change only slows the rate of increase in atmospheric concentrations of GHGs, with currently unknown consequences.

     8. Effective international mitigation policy for either problem may also require substantial technological change in a wide range of industries. It is prob-

able that some social change will be required to mitigate climate change (Intergovernmental Panel on Climate Change 1995).

9. MacNeill et al. (1991) uses the concept of a "shadow ecology" to illustrate the cross-border ecological impacts of consumption and production choices primarily in the developed countries. As the poorer countries develop, their shadow ecologies will expand.

10. Transnational corporations headquartered and with substantial operations in developed countries often require their subsidiaries in LDCs to maintain the same advanced environmental practices applied in their "home" country. For example, see Levy (1995).

11. Because of low transportation costs, global resource markets draw resources from wherever they are located. Product standards in developed countries also bias the choice of technology throughout the world. In LDCs, different relative factor pricing (between labor and capital) make technologies different from those of the developed countries rational choices (Bhalla 1985). However, less technologically advanced industrialization often consumes more natural goods per capita and per unit of production (i.e., they are less eco-efficient).

12. Although the treaty establishing the World Trade Organization (WTO) includes provision for environmental protection, the overriding purpose of the organization is to reduce restrictions on free trade. The effect of free trade on the environment is unclear and much debated: global competition may increase eco-efficiency or trade may merely spread ecologically destructive techniques. However, as argued in chapters 3 and 4, there is little reason to suppose that free markets, whether local or global, will always protect eco-systems.

13. Many environmentalists believe that, in the absence of (or in addition to) external direction of consumer choices as through price signals, making consumers aware of the environmental effects of their consumption choices will encourage them to make less environmentally damaging choices. The problems of changing beliefs and values through education is discussed in more detail in chapter 7 and 8.

14. In the negotiations for a climate convention, the industrialized countries have argued that technology will reduce GHG emissions; but they simultaneously have rejected subsidized transfer of such technology to LDCs and increased development aid (from my notes of meetings 2 and 4 of the Negotiating Committee for a Framework Convention on Climate Change at Geneva in June and December 1991 and the Second Conference of the Parties to the United Nations Framework Convention on Climate Change in Geneva in June 1996).

15. For most purposes, international institutions are equivalent to international regimes defined as "principles, norms, rules, and decision-making procedures around which actor expectations converge in a given issue-area" (Krasner 1983). Regimes may or may not be reflected in a formal treaty or even in a formal organization such as the International Whaling Commission.

16. The very vagueness of the term *interests*, comparable to the term *preferences* in economics, makes it very unlikely that researching interest formation will help to satisfactorily describe, explain, or predict state behaviors.

17. Because in security issues the preservation of the state is largely a self-evident interest, once an issue becomes understood as a matter of national security, outcome preferences are relatively uncontentious.

18. Multiple plays of a prisoner's dilemma game may produce cooperation. A "tit-for-tat" strategy in which, in each round, a player responds with a comparable behavior to that of the other player in the previous round, encourages cooperation and punishes defection (Keohane and Axelrod 1986; Axelrod 1984).

19. At the initiation of negotiations on climate change, states were unsure of their own preferences because of the scientific uncertainty, but they also were unsure of the preferences of other states. Major players such as the United States and the United Kingdom have taken radically different positions between ozone depletion and climate change; even the Montreal Protocol on Ozone Depleting Substances was not a strong predictor of action on global warming.

20. As Ruggie (1983) has suggested, there is an "embedded liberalism" in the global political economy, even more now than in the 1980s, that rewards beliefs that are consonant with its hegemony.

21. Historical materialist worldviews also assert that the structure of the international socioeconomic system and a country's position therein determine its behavior (Wallerstein 1979; Gunder Frank 1969; Chase-Dunn 1981; Palma 1978). Developed countries will be unable to act outside their structurally determined role of exploiter. Paterson (1996) argues that historical materialist analysis offers an explanation of the climate change negotiations through 1992 that is at least as effective as any other.

22. The developed countries have argued that global efficiency would be optimized if the UNFCCC were implemented "jointly." This provision permits developed countries to take credit against any future emissions target for their firms' implementation of projects that reduce GHG emissions in developing countries. Developing countries believe that this will permit the developed countries to shuffle off much of their responsibility for climate change mitigation by using a form of technological colonialism.

23. Such issues are more likely to result in "multilateralism," defined as an international institution representing generalized principles of conduct that emphasize nondiscrimination, indivisibility, and "diffuse reciprocity" (Ruggie 1992, 571; Cowhey 1993; Keohane 1985).

24. Rent is an excess over the normal profit available to a producer in a fully competitive market. "Rent-seeking" is sometimes thought of as unproductive activity in search of extraordinary gain.

25. Learning results from a recognition that old structures and patterns of behavior are incapable of solving the problem. Adaptation, a more incremental change in the state's preferences, is a change in the means of action rather than ends, and it occurs within a stable framework constructed on a static belief system (Haas 1983; Sandholtz 1989).

26. It is evident that constructivist theory in international relations somewhat mirrors the development of communitarian political theories. However, constructivist theorists do not explicitly make this connection. There are a number of strands of constructivist theory. A rule-based approach (Onuf 1989; Kubalkova et al. 1998) that is considered by many scholars to be out in left field may be the most fruitful for theorizing about the politics of the international environment and of sustainable development.

27. Many ENGOs such as the Friends of the Earth, Greenpeace, and the World Wildlife Fund have globalized as fast as TNCs. They are directly represented in many countries around the world or are allied with local activist groups and are thus able to disseminate ideas and activities globally through their own networks of grassroots activists.

28. ENGOs and TNCs are also able to influence negotiations on international environmental policy by lobbying delegates and through close contacts with intergovernmental organizations such as the United Nations Environment Programme or the United Nations Development Program. Most developed states and some LDCs meet regularly with ENGOs and industrial representatives on international environmental issues such as climate change (Harrison 1994).

29. At the climate change negotiations, there are often nearly as many NGO delegates as delegates from participating states. Of the NGO delegates, ENGO delegates usually are more numerous than the delegates from industrial lobby groups.

30. An intergovernmental organization is an international institution that has a physical presence in the form of offices, employees, desks, office equipment, and so on.

31. In the United States, Pat Buchanan and Ross Perot exemplify this argument. Orthodox trade theory for nearly two centuries (Ricardo 1960) has asserted that freeing global markets by reducing all restraints on international trade will benefit all countries involved.

## CHAPTER 7. A PROBLEM OF CONSCIOUSNESS

1. Ecology is "the study of 'life at home' with emphasis on 'the totality or pattern of relations between organisms and their environment.' . . . Although ecology remains strongly rooted in biology, it has emerged from biology as an essentially new integrative discipline that links physical and biological processes and the social sciences" (Odum 1983, 1–3).

2. As Dobson (1995, 9–11) comments, "ecocentric politics explicitly seeks to decentre the human being . . . to refuse to believe that the world was made for human beings."

3. Management of ecosystems presupposes a defined purpose and a sufficient understanding of the complex relations within the ecosystem and between it and other ecosystems. The purpose usually is to create ecosystems that are conducive to human development or that humans value as "natural." But, ecosystems managed by humans are virtual representations of natural ones. Only invaded systems require management. The re-introduction of wolves into Yellowstone Park may have been intended to control bison and elk populations naturally. With the annual millions of (car borne) visitors to the area, any "natural" equilibrium can only be artificial, a human construct to appease aesthetic sensibilities. The difficulty in managing ecosystems is not only knowing *how*, but also in deciding *why*, to what end.

4. Dobson uses the term *ecologism* for the collection of ideas and theories that underpins the ethics narrative. This contrasts with Paehlke's (1989) "environmentalism."

5. Ethics and morality are linked but distinct concepts. "The institution of morality is particularly concerned with duties that arise from the rules or precepts that constitute it, whereas the ethical realm also includes a concern with ideals and ends that go beyond these duties, and especially with *the outcomes of action*" (Nardin 1992, 3–4; emphasis added). While "morality is . . . the effort to guide one's conduct by reason—that is, to do what there are the best reasons for doing—while giving equal weights to the interests of each individual who will be affected by one's conduct" (Rachels 1986, 11), ethics seeks more practical solutions to the question of how one should live in the environment in which one finds oneself. Where moral philosophy prescribes abstract rules of right behavior, ethics looks to the arguments that weigh values in the context of reality.

6. The nature of rationality is contestable. Kant thought of human rationality as a human freedom to act in a selfless, non-egotistical, or disinterested fashion and not as the result of reason, language, or intelligence. Kant argues that humans have rights as rational beings and duties to other rational beings to treat them as ends and not as means. An act is moral only if the actor wills that act for all rational beings (DesJardins 1992, 33–35, Miller 1993, 392–410). In contrast, the rational economic actor is individually self-optimizing. Although that might include altruistic acts, it is not expected to unless they satisfy some desire of the actor. That is, altruistic behaviors can be assumed to satisfy an unknown desire. Because nonhumans cannot communicate their interests does not mean that those interests do not exist nor that they should be ignored. It is not necessary to impute rationality to argue that nonhumans have interests in continued life or legal rights. Is it reasonable to assume their interests are comparable to human interests or would some of the creatures in the Mineral King Valley welcome development because they see a benefit in it that humans do not?

7. If values are indistinguishable from interests, the interests of others can be ignored (Ferry 1995, 41). Ferry also recounts at some length the laws instituted in Nazi Germany to protect animal rights.

8. A small community anchored to its local ecosystem would be more practical in Tallahassee than Timbuktu, because of differences in climate and human and natural capital.

9. If women are uniquely able to appreciate and empathize with nature and men are equally but differently biologically determined, about half of the human race would seem to be permanently alienated from nature. Apparently, the hope must lie in a general acceptance of caring among both men and women.

10. Some historians argue that it was adoption of agriculture, which was predominantly then as it still is in many LDCs an aspect of the feminine, that first gave humans command over nature. From agriculture grew increasing technology, military capability, and urban environments isolated from nature (Keegan 1994). Though hunter-gatherer tribes such as the Native American tribes that lived on the huge bison herds of the North American plains were male dominated, they are generally considered environmentally benign. Yet, "archaeologists say the idea of noble savage protecting the environment is a myth." Humans, whether male or female or from a patriarchal or matriarchal society, seem always to have despoiled nature (Stone 1993, 239 n.5).

11. As consequences are related to context, utilitarianism offers no absolute or universal ethic; murder may be appropriate if as a result of the action the greatest happiness of the greatest number results. The plot to murdering Hitler in 1943, if it had succeeded, would have been a moral act because of the large number of lives that would probably have been saved.

12. One might expect that the aesthetic utility of each spotted owl will increase as their numbers decrease. A small number of (endangered) spotted owls in zoos may be of more aesthetic utility than a flock spread through the woods of Oregon. If so, under utilitarianism without consideration of the utility of all sentient animals, decimation of their numbers would be beneficial.

13. Not only the individual human possessor of land is morally considerable, but also the extended community of humans and other members of the ecosystem that is rooted in the land.

14. The land ethic is a critique of the progressive conservationalism or "wise use" movement that was the dominant environmental paradigm in the United States at the time Leopold wrote his book. Under wise use, the natural environment is a bundle of resources to be used most efficiently to satisfy the needs of the majority of humans alive now. As advocated by Gifford Pinchot, it rested on three principles: first, development of natural resources should be for those now living; second, it must minimize waste of natural resources; and finally, it must be for the benefit of the many not the few (Taylor 1992, 56, 20).

15. These rules are hierarchically ordered. The first is a negative duty rather than an obligation to assist an organism in the pursuit of its purpose. This requires that humans not "try to manipulate, control, modify, or 'manage' natural ecosystems or otherwise intervene in their normal functioning" (Taylor 1986, 175). Only if "significant good can result without permanent harm" would restitutive justice be superior to the other rules (DesJardins 1992, 158). Where humans' interests conflict with the interests of other organisms, humans may pursue their interests only in self-defense. Other rules prevent unrecompensed exploitation of weaker species. The rule of proportionality prevents the human's pursuit of their nonbasic interests at the expense of another organism's basic interests; the rule of minimum wrong requires us to minimize any harm to nonhumans that cannot be avoided; and a requirement for distributive justice ensures that humans accept an equal share of any benefits or costs. Where human and nonhuman interests conflict and the prior rules have not prevented harm to nonhumans, the balance of justice is achieved through restitution.

16. The focus on a duty of care to individual organisms also creates a logical problem. By commenting that "our demise would be no loss to other species," Taylor (1988) opposes his essential perspective that humans are integral to the web of life. But removal of the boundary between human and nonhuman life "blurs the distinction between ourselves and other living things so crucial for locating such boundaries," and the conflicts between humans and other organisms that he considers inevitable will become more difficult to identify and to rectify (Taylor 1992, 115–125).

17. Inflicting unnecessary cruelty or pain on higher animals can rouse strong human emotions. For example, see "Also a Part of Creation," on protests about exports of certain animals from Britain. An argument that maltreatment of animals is "inhumane" means that humans are diminished by the action.

18. "What is crucial in making things valuable . . . is the fact that they have a history of having been created by natural processes rather than by artificial human ones." These processes extend to the solar system and the universe (Goodin 1992, 26–27).

19. Bob Pepperman Taylor (1992) also correctly comments that arguments for intrinsic valuation usually rely on appeals to intuition rather than reasoned arguments.

20. Deep ecologists and bioregionalists (or social ecologists) agree on the general nature of the problem, but differ in their solutions. For both schools of thought, alienated humans are environmentally destructive, and a closer awareness of nature, and sense of connection to it, would permit them to realize their true selves. Deep ecologists are speaking to individuals about the need to reorder their thinking patterns; but social ecologists are emphasizing the effect of a better, more just social organization on the human psyche, demonstrating their Marxian connections. Disagreements between deep and social ecologists are sometimes remindful of the virulence of the factional intrigues that occurred

within the Central Committee of the Soviet Communist Party. For example, Sessions places Bookchin close to the hated technocratic New Age Movement (Sessions 1995) and Murray Bookchin has often criticized aspects of deep ecological thought.

21. The belief common to all green theories is that human consciousness must be adapted to the reality of the holistic, systemic character of nature of which humans are a part. Ethical arguments built upon the inherent worth of, or an intrinsic value in, nonhumans, philosophies of self-actualization through proper relations with the nonhuman world, or spiritual acceptance of a oneness with the rest of nature, each is targeted at the consciousness of position within a natural system of individual humans and nonhumans.

22. It is often argued that a better understanding of the issues will improve decision making (Ophuls and Boyan 1992: National Commission 1993; Milbrath 1989). Thus, the importance of technical experts in policy making. However, this better understanding is inevitably limited to collecting data (the science project) rather than examining the beliefs and values that humans hold and do not regularly re-examine.

23. Many organized religions, by turning attention to a heaven and away from earthly pursuits are, at best, agnostic about green values and at worst, opposed to diminishing human stature to one equal to the rest of creation.

24. For example, Reuters reported on September 17, 1998, that the German Green Party was "riven between moderate and radical factions." As a result of this internal debate, its manifesto "first included and dropped some radical policies such as trebling the price of petrol through higher taxes." In the hope of winning electoral gains, the final manifesto was quite moderate. It included quite marginal changes in income taxes, proposals to make labor cheaper and energy more expensive, closure of all nuclear power stations, and reform of the state pension scheme financed through a private wealth tax.

25. Greenpeace and other grassroots environmental organizations have become skilled at using salient single issues to mobilize popular thought and activity through media coverage. By some measures, more than two-thirds of the citizens of most countries are concerned about the environment (Dunlap, Gallup, and Gallup 1993), in part because of ENGO activities.

26. Although social scientists seek to define the causes of human behaviour in groups, they assume a fixed and generalizable human nature when attempting to explain social behavior.

## CHAPTER 8. POLICY PRINCIPLES FOR SUSTAINABLE DEVELOPMENT

1. Brewer and deLeon (1983) offer the textbook view. In Lindblom (1959 and 1980) goals are incremental, and Simon (1972) stresses the inability to include all possible alternatives. Kingdon (1984), and to a lesser extent Polsby (1984), note the chaotic and chance nature of agenda-setting and policy selection.

2. The interpretations in the dominant policy narratives reflect well-entrenched voices of what may be called capitalist apologists, liberal institutionalists, and critics of the status quo.

3. Reductionism assumes that the whole can be defined in terms of simple rules for the arrangement of parts. If that were true, the study of living systems would only require the disciplines of chemistry and physics, because all living organisms are made of the same atoms and molecules. A bicycle can be defined in terms of its components and the structure imposed on those parts by the manufacturer. However, life appears to be an emergent property of the self-organizing interaction between atoms and molecules. Because the parts are self-organizing there is a degree of order (Kauffman 1995) but the structure and behavior of the system cannot be absolutely predicted. Thus, life cannot be defined in terms of an iron law governing the structure of atoms and molecules within a living system. It may be understood as the spontaneous order emerging from the interaction between atoms and molecules that is governed by only generalized rules of behavior for the parts within the system.

4. I use the term *community* to mean any ordered group of humans in physical proximity who actively interact in the pursuit of a common purpose. Examples of communities would be towns, cities, countries, etc.

5. If all humans viewed themselves as part of a community, albeit a community within which there is disagreement over facts and values, political discourse could be socially constructive while increasing participation in decision making. Those who would label such notions "unrealistic idealism" should remember that the future reflects ideals. Because realism is the acceptance and reification of what is, however bad or stupid, only idealists who hope for change toward a better future are truly realistic.

6. The tricycle is not a completely closed system but may be treated as one because all relevant forces including air resistance and the gravitational pull of Mars may be included in the calculations.

7. Of course, this is the collective action problem that rational choice theorists such as Olson (1965) have identified but failed to solve.

8. Two examples with different purposes are Carley and Christie (1993) and the National Commission on the Environment (1993).

9. Many types of steel can be manufactured in small plants instead of vast foundries and rolling mills. Improvements in systems for transporting both parts and control information have permitted the physical dispersion of manufacturing. Products from cars to computers are assembled from parts manufactured by a number of firms dispersed around the world.

10. Taxation is generally favored by economists as being a more efficient form of behavioral redirection than regulatory policies, creating less drag on the economy. The problem with such green taxes would be their regressive nature.

However, progressive green taxation could be achieved in a number of ways, including the return of greater amounts of government services to the poor. With globalization of commerce and the increase in electronic financial and commercial transactions, governments should welcome the opportunity to shift the burden of taxation to physical goods and processes from the chimera of "income" and "profit."

11. Efforts have begun to establish a requirement for green auditing. These include ISO 14000, British Standard 7750 (now superseded) and The European Union's Eco-Management and Audit Scheme. Many transnational corporations require (usually internal) auditing of environmental management plans and practices. For examples of academic discussion of the problems of measuring environmental performance, see Bennett, James, and Klinkers (1998). Truly effective green auditing would require quantitative measures of eco-efficiency comparable to the financial requirements set out in generally accepted accounting principles. Correcting the bias in national accounts against recording the full cost of natural goods (see chapter 3) would pressure governments toward more sustainable economic policies (see Daly and Cobb 1989 for one way to correct GDP errors).

12. In less developed countries, taxation is often disproportionately imposed on imports and other activities (such as licenses) that may be more directly monitored by government officials. The weakness of many LDC governments prevents them from collecting taxes on income and capital from the few rich or the many poor citizens. A tax on natural goods usage would also be difficult for them to monitor.

13. A school teacher I once knew used to say that "good manners is consideration for other people," a good rule of thumb for appropriate behavior in a complex and mobile society. This echoes Smith's (1976) "sympathy" and similar ideals discussed in chapter 5. The market encourages such thinking only in terms of material reward for satisfaction of others' material wants.

14. As Schumpeter (see Freeman 1992, 79) has commented of technological innovation, stringing horse-drawn mail coaches together does not make a train. There is a distinct difference between the two phenomena.

# REFERENCES

"A Bug with Social Aspirations." *The Economist* 344, 8030 (August 16, 1997):25.

Adler, Emmanuel, and Peter M. Haas. 1992. "Conclusion: Epistemic Communities, World Order, and the Creation of a Reflective Research Program." *International Organization* 46, no. 1 (Winter):367–390.

Allegré, Claude J., and Stephen H. Schneider. 1994. "The Evolution of the Earth." *Scientific American* 271, 4 (October 1994):66–75.

Almond, Gabriel. 1990. *A Discipline Divided: Schools and Sects in Political Science.* Newbury Park, CA: Sage Publications.

"Also a Part of Creation." *The Economist* 335, 7928 (19 August, 1995):19–21.

Anderson, Terry L. 1995. "Water Options for the Blue Planet." In *The True State of the Planet.* Edited by Ronald Bailey. New York: The Free Press.

Arendt, Hannah. 1958. *The Human Condition.* Chicago: University of Chicago Press.

Aristotle. *Politics.* Trans. B. Jowett. Reprint, Oxford: Clarendon Press, 1885.

Arndt, H.W. 1993. "Review Article: Sustainable Development and the Discount Rate." *Economic Development and Cultural Change* (1 April):651–661.

Arrhenius, Svante. 1896. "On the Influence of Carbonic Acid in the Air Upon Temperature of the Ground." *Philosophic Magazine* 41:237–276.

Arrow, Kenneth J. 1951. *Social Choice and Individual Values.* New York: John Wiley & Sons, Inc.

———. 1962. "Economic Welfare and the Allocation of Resources for Invention." In *The Rate and Direction of Inventive Activity: Economic and Social Factors.* Edited by Universities-National Bureau Committee of Economic Research. Princeton: Princeton University Press.

Arthur, W. Brian. 1988. "Self-Reinforcing Mechanisms in Economics." In *The Economy as an Evolving Complex System: The Proceedings of the Evolutionary Paths of the Global Economy Workshop, held September, 1987 in Santa Fe New Mexico.* Edited by Philip W. Anderson, Kenneth J. Arrow and David Pines. Redwood City, CA: Addison-Wesley.

———. 1990. "Positive Feedbacks in the Economy." *Scientific American* (February):92–99.

Avery, Dennis. 1995. "Saving the Planet with Pesticides: Increasing Food Supplies While Preserving the Earth's Biodiversity." In *The True State of the Planet*. Edited by Ronald Bailey. New York: The Free Press.

Axelrod, Robert. 1984. *The Evolution of Cooperation*. New York: Basic Books.

Ayres, Robert U. 1985. "A Schumpeterian Model of Technological Substitution." *Technology Forecasting and Social Change* 27:375–383.

Bailey, Ronald, ed. 1995. *The True State of the Planet*. New York: The Free Press.

Balling, Robert C., Jr. 1992. *The Heated Debate: Greenhouse Predictions Versus Climate Reality*. San Francisco: Pacific Research Institute for Public Policy.

Barbier, Edward B. 1987. "The Concept of Sustainable Economic Development." *Environmental Conservation* 14, 2 (Summer):101–110.

———, ed. 1993. *Economics and Ecology: New Frontiers and Sustainable Development*. New York: Chapman & Hall.

Barbour, Michael G. 1995. "Ecological Fragmentation in the Fifties." In *Uncommon Ground: Toward Reinventing Nature*. Edited by William Cronon. New York: W. W. Norton.

Barry, Brian. 1989. *Liberty and Justice: Essays in Political Theory 2*. Oxford: Clarendon Press.

Barry, Norman P. 1989. *An Introduction to Modern Political Theory*. 2nd ed. New York: St. Martin's Press.

Bass, Bernard M. 1981. *Stogdill's Handbook of Leadership: A Survey of Theory and Research*. New York: The Free Press.

Becker, Robert A. 1982. "Intergenerational Equity: The Capital-Environment Trade-off." *Journal of Environmental Economics and Management* 9:165–185.

Bellah, Robert N., Richard Madsen, William M. Sullivan, Ann Swidler, and Steven M. Tipton. 1985. *Habits of the Heart: Individualism and Commitment in American Life*. New York: Harper & Row.

Benedick, Richard Elliot. 1991. *Ozone Diplomacy: New Directions in Safeguarding the Planet*. Cambridge MA: Harvard University Press.

Bennett, Martin, Peter James, and Leon Klinkers. 1998. "Special Issue." *Greener Management International*, Issue 21, Spring 1998.

Bentham, Jeremy. 1948. *Principles of Morals and Legislation*. New York: Hafner.

Bernal, J. D. 1989. "After Twenty-Five Years: A Reprint of the 1964 paper by J D Bernal." *Science and Public Policy* 16, 3 (June):143–151.

Bernauer, Thomas and Peter Moser. 1996. "Reducing Pollution of the River Rhine: The Influence of International Cooperation." *Journal of Environment and Development* 5, no. 4 (December):389–415.

Best, Steven, and Douglas Kellner. 1997. *The Postmodern Turn*. New York: The Guildford Press.

Bhalla, A. S. 1985. *Technology and Employment in Industry: A Case Study Approach*. 3rd ed. Geneva: International Labor Office.

Bhalla, A. S., and James Dilmus, eds. 1988. *New Technologies and Development: Experiences in "Technology Blending."* Boulder: Lynne Rienner Publishers.

Bishop, Jerry E. 1994. "New Silicon Cell can Halve Cost of Solar Energy." *The Wall Street Journal* (19 January):B7.

Blaney, David L. 1996. "Reconceptualizing Autonomy: The Difference Dependency Theory Makes." *Review of International Political Economy* 3, 3 (Autumn):459–497.

Blegan, Bryce. 1988, "International Cooperation in Protection of Atmospheric Ozone: The Montreal Protocol on Substances that Deplete the Ozone Layer." *Denver Journal of International Law and Policy* 16:413–428.

Bookchin, Murray. 1986. *The Modern Crisis.* Philadelphia: New Society Publishing.

Bowden, Gary. 1985. "The Social Construction of Validity in Estimates of US Crude Oil Reserves." *Social Studies of Science* 15, 2 (May):207–240.

Bozeman, Barry, and Albert N. Link. 1984. "Tax Incentives for R&D: A Critical Evaluation." *Research Policy* 13, 1 (February):21–31.

Braidotti, Rosi, Ewa Charkiewicz, Sabine Haüsler, and Saskia Wieringa. 1994. *Women, the Environment and Sustainable Development: Towards a Theoretical Synthesis.* London: Zed Books, in association with INSTRAW.

Brewer, Gary D., and Peter deLeon. 1983. *The Foundations of Policy Analysis.* Homewood, IL: Dorsey Press.

"Brain Damage." *The Economist* 327, 7807 (17 April, 1993):56–57.

Bronfenbrenner, Martin, Werner Sichel, and Wayland Gardner. 1987. *Macroeconomics.* 2nd ed. Boston: Houghton Mifflin.

Brown, Lester R., ed. 1991. *The World Watch Reader on Global Environmental Issues.* New York: W. W. Norton.

———. 1992a. "Launching the Environmental Revolution." In *State of the World 1992,* edited by Lester R. Brown. New York: W. W. Norton.

———. ed. 1992b. *State of the World 1992.* New York: W. W. Norton.

Brown, Lester R., Christopher Flavin, and Sandra Postel. 1991. "Vision of a Sustainable World." In *The WorldWatch Reader on Global Environmental Issues.* Edited by Lester R. Brown. New York: W. W. Norton.

Brown, Lester R., Nicholas Lenssen, and Hal Kane. 1995. *Vital Signs 1995: The Trends that Are Shaping Our Future.* New York: W. W. Norton, for the Worldwatch Institute.

Brown, Mark B., Wert Canzler, Frank Fischer, and Andreas Knie. 1995. "Technological Innovation Through Environmental Policy: California's Zero-Emission Vehicle Regulation." *Public Productivity & Management Review* 19, 1 (September):77–93.

Brown, William M. 1984. "The Outlook for Future Petroleum Supplies." In *The Resourceful Earth: A Response to Global 2000.* Edited by Julian L. Simon and Herman Kahn. New York: Basil Blackwell.

Brundtland, Gro Harlem. 1989. "Sustainable Development: An Overview." *Development—Journal of SID* 2/3:13–14.

Burton, John W. 1972. *World Society.* Cambridge: Cambridge University Press.

Cairncross, Frances. 1989. "Costing the Earth: A Survey of the Environment." *The Economist* 313, 7619 (2 September).

———. 1992. *Costing the Earth: The Challenge for Governments, the Opportunities for Business.* Boston: Harvard Business School Press.

Caldwell, Lynton Keith. 1990. *International Environmental Policy: Emergence and Dimensions.* 2nd ed. Durham, NC: Duke University Press.

Calvin, William H. 1994. "The Emergence of Intelligence." *Scientific American* 271, 4 (October 1994):101–107.

Campbell, Colin J., and Jean H. Laherrère. "The End of Cheap Oil." *Scientific American* 278, 3 (March 1998):77–83.

Campbell, T. D. 1971. *Adam Smith's Science of Morals.* London: George Allen & Unwin.

"Capitalism's Creative Destruction." *The Economist* 323, 7753 (4 April, 1992):15.

Caporaso, James A. 1992. "International Relations Theory and Multilateralism: The Search for Foundations." *International Organization* 46, no. 3 (Summer):599–630.

Capra, Fritjof. 1996. *The Web of Life: A New Scientific Understanding of Living Systems.* New York: Anchor Books.

Carew-Reid, Jeremy, Robert Prescott-Allen, Stephen Bass, and Barry Dalal-Clayton. 1994. *Strategies for National Sustainable Development: A Handbook for their Planning and Implementation.* London: Earthscan Publications, in association with The World Conservation Union and the International Institute for Environment and Development.

Carley, Michael, and Ian Christie. 1993. *Managing Sustainable Development.* Minneapolis: University of Minnesota Press.

Carr, Edward Hallett. 1951. *The Twenty Years' Crisis.* London: Macmillan and Co.

Chacko, George T. 1991. *Decision-Making Under Uncertainty: An Applied Statistics Approach.* New York: Praeger.

Chase-Dunn, Christopher. 1981. "Interstate Systems and Capitalist World-Economy: One Logic or Two?" *International Studies Quarterly* 25, 1 (March):19–42.

Clammer, John, ed. 1987. *Beyond the New Economic Anthropology.* New York: St. Martin's Press.

Cleveland, Cutler J. 1991. "Natural Resource Scarcity and Economic Growth Revisited: Economic and Biophysical Perspectives." In *Ecological Economics: The Science and Management of Sustainability.* Edited by Robert Costanza. New York: Columbia University Press.

Cline, William. 1992. *The Economics of Global Warming.* Washington, DC: Institute for International Economics.

Coates, Geoffrey H. 1993. "Facilitating Sustainable Development: Role of Engineer." *Journal of Professional Issues in Engineering Education and Practice* 119, 3 (July):225–229.

Commoner, Barry. 1971. *The Closing Circle: Nature, Man, and Technology.* New York: Alfred A. Knopf.

Cooke, Roger M. 1991. *Experts in Uncertainty: Opinion and Subjective Probability.* New York: Oxford University Press.

Cooper, Richard N. 1968. *The Economics of Interdependence: Economic Policy in the Atlantic Community.* New York: McGraw-Hill.

"Costa Nature." *The Economist* 322, 7740 (4 January, 1992):38.

Costanza, Robert, Herman E. Daly, and Joy A. Bartholomew. 1991. "Goals, Agenda, and Policy Recommendations for Ecological Economics." In *Ecological Economics: The Science and Management of Sustainability*. Edited by Robert Costanza. New York: Columbia University Press.

Cottell, Michael N. T. 1993. "Facilitating Sustainable Development: Is Our Approach Correct?" *Journal of Professional Issues in Engineering Education and Practice* 119, 3 (July):220–224.

Cowhey, Peter F. 1993. "Domestic Institutions and the Credibility of International Commitments: Japan and the United States." *International Organization* 47, 2 (Spring):299–326.

Crotty, William. 1993. *The Theory and Practice of Political Science*. Edited by William Crotty. Evanston: Northwestern University Press.

Cyert, Richard M., and David C. Mowery. 1989. "Technology, Employment and U.S. Competitiveness." *Scientific American* 260, 5 (May):54–62.

Dahl, Robert A., and Charles E. Lindblom. 1953. *Politics, Economics, and Welfare*. New York: Harper Brothers.

Daly, Herman E. 1991. "Elements of Environmental Macroeconomics." In *Ecological Economics: The Science and Management of Sustainability*. Edited by Robert Costanza. New York: Columbia University Press.

———. 1991. *Steady-State Economics*. 2nd ed. Washington, DC: Island Press.

———. 1993. "The Steady-State Economy: Toward a Political Economy of Biophysical Equilibrium and Moral Growth." In *Valuing the Earth*. Edited by Herman E. Daly and Kenneth N Townsend. Cambridge, MA: MIT Press.

Daly, Herman E., and John B. Cobb, Jr. 1989. *For the Common Good: Redirecting the Economy toward Community, the Environment, and a Sustainable Future*. Boston: Beacon Press.

Daly, Herman E., and Kenneth N. Townsend. 1993. "Introduction to *Essays Toward a Steady-State Economy*." In *Valuing the Earth*. Edited by Herman E. Daly and Kenneth N. Townsend. Cambridge, MA: MIT Press.

———, eds. 1993. *Valuing the Earth: Economics, Ecology, Ethics*. Cambridge, MA/London: MIT Press.

Daly, Mary. 1987. *Gyn/Ecology*. London: The Women's Press.

David, Paul A. 1975. *Technical Choice Innovation and Economic Growth*. Cambridge: Cambridge University Press.

———. 1985. "Clio and the Economics of QWERTY." *The American Economic Review* 75, 2 (May):332–337.

d'Entrèves, Maurizio Passerin. 1990. "Communitarianism and the Question of Tolerance." *Journal of Social Philosophy* 21, 1 (Spring):77–91.

Dery, David. 1984. *Problem Definition in Policy Analysis*. Lawrence, KS: University of Kansas Press.

DesJardins, Joseph R. 1992. *Environmental Ethics: An Introduction to Environmental Philosophy*. Belmont, California: Wadsworth.

Devall, Bill, and George Sessions. 1985. *Deep Ecology: Living as if Nature Mattered*. Salt Lake City: Gibbs Smith.

Dickson, David. 1974. *The Politics of Alternative Technology.* New York: Universe Books.

Diesing, Paul. 1982. *Science and Ideology in the Policy Sciences.* New York: Aldine.

DiLorenzo, Thomas J. 1993. "The Mirage of Sustainable Development." *The Futurist* (September–October):14–19.

Dobson, Andrew. 1995. *Green Political Thought.* 2nd ed. London: Routledge.

Dodge, Jim. 1981. "Living by Life: Some Bioregional Theory and Practice." *The CoEvolution Quarterly* 32 (Winter):6–12.

Dosi, Giovanni. 1982. "Technological Paradigms and Technological Trajectories: A Suggested Interpretation of the Determinants and Directions of Technical Change." *Research Policy* 11, 3 (June):147–162.

Dotto, Lydia, and Harold Schiff. 1978. *The Ozone War.* New York: Doubleday.

Dryzek, John S. 1996. "Foundations for Environmental Political Economy: The Search for *Homo Ecologicus.*" *New Political Economy* 1, 1 (March):27–40.

———. 1997. *The Politics of the Earth: Environmental Discourses.* Oxford: Oxford University Press.

Dworkin, Ronald. 1981. "What Is Equality? Part I: Equality of Welfare; Part II: Equality of Resources." *Philosophy and Public Affairs* 10, 3–4: 185–246 and 283–345.

———. 1985. *A Matter of Principle.* London: Harvard University Press.

Easton, David. 1953. *The Political System.* New York: Knopf.

Eberstadt, Nicholas. 1995. "Population, Food, and Income: Global Trends in the Twentieth Century." In *The True State of the Planet.* Edited by Ronald Bailey. New York: The Free Press.

"Economic Miracle or Myth?" *The Economist* 329, 7831 (2 October, 1993):41–42.

Ehrlich, Paul R. 1968. *The Population Bomb.* New York: Ballantine, for the Sierra Club.

Ehrlich, Paul R., and Anne Ehrlich. 1974. *The End of Affluence.* Rivercity, MA: Riversity Press.

———. 1991. *Healing the Planet: Strategies for Resolving the Environmental Crisis.* Reading, MA: Addison-Wesley.

———. 1992. "The Value of Biodiversity." *Ambio* 21, 3 (May):219–226.

"The Electric Car's Achilles' Axle." *The Economist* 324, 7777 (19 September, 1992):101–102.

Elster, Jon. 1983. *Explaining Technical Change.* Cambridge, England: Cambridge University Press.

———. 1986. "Introduction." In *Rational Choice.* Edited by Jon Elster. New York: New York University Press.

Etzioni, Amitai, ed. 1995. *Rights and the Common Good: The Communitarian Perspective.* New York: St. Martin's Press.

Evans, Judy. 1993. "Ecofeminism and the Politics of the Gendered Self." In *The Politics of Nature: Explorations in Green Political Theory.* Edited by Andrew Dobson and Paul Lucardie. London: Routledge.

Evans, Peter B., Harold K. Jacobson, and Robert D. Putnam, eds. 1993. *Double-Edged Diplomacy: Institutional Bargaining and Domestic Politics.* Berkeley: University of California Press.

"Evo-Economics: Biology Meets the Dismal Science." *The Economist* 329, 7843 (25 December, 1993), 93–95.

Farman, J. C., B. G. Gardiner, and J. D. Shanklin. 1985. "Large Losses of Total Ozone in Antarctic Reveal Seasonal CLOx/NOx Interaction." *Letter to Nature, Nature* 315 (16 May).

Ferry, Luc. 1995. *The New Ecological Order.* Chicago: University of Chicago Press.

Field, Barry C. 1994. *Environmental Economics: An Introduction.* New York: McGraw-Hill.

Fields, Gary S. 1980. *Poverty, Inequality, and Development.* Cambridge: Cambridge University Press.

"First, Ask the Locals." *The Economist* 336, 7939 (4 November, 1995):28.

"For Richer, For Poorer." *The Economist* 333, 7888 (5 November, 1994):19–21.

Forgacs, David. 1988. *An Antonio Gramsci Reader: Selected Writings 1916–1935.* New York: Schocken Books.

Foucault, Michel. 1977. *Discipline and Punishment: The Birth of a Prison.* New York: Pantheon.

———. 1980. *Power/Knowledge.* New York: Pantheon.

———. 1982. "The Subject and Power." In *Michel Foucault: Beyond Structuralism and Hermeneutics.* Edited by Herbert Dreyfus and Paul Rabinow. Chicago: University of Chicago Press.

———. 1984. "Truth and Power." In *The Foucault Reader.* Edited by Paul Rabinow. New York: Pantheon.

———. 1991. "Questions of Method." In *The Foucault Effect: Studies in Governmentality.* Edited by Graham Burchell, Colin Gordon, and Peter Miller. Chicago: The University of Chicago Press.

Freeman, Christopher. 1977. "Economics of Research and Development." In *Science, Technology, and Society: A Cross-Disciplinary Perspective.* Edited by I. Spiegel-Rosing and David deS. Price. London: Sage Publications.

———. 1979. "The Determinants of Innovation: Market Demand, Technology, and the Response to Social Problems." *Futures* 11 (June):206–215.

———. 1992. *The Economics of Hope: Essays on Technical Change, Economic Growth, and the Environment.* London: Pinter Publishers.

Freeman, Donald M. 1991. "The Making of a Discipline." In *The Theory and Practice of Political Science.* Edited by William Crotty. Evanston: Northwestern University Press.

Friedman, Milton. 1962. *Capitalism and Freedom.* Chicago: The University of Chicago Press.

"From Major to Minor." *The Economist* 339, 7966 (18 May, 1996):63–64.

Frosch, Robert A. 1995. "The Industrial Ecology of the 21st Century." *Scientific American* 273, 3 (September):178–181.

Fukuyama, Francis. 1992. *The End of History and The Last Man.* New York: Free Press.

Funtowicz, Silvio O., and Jerome R. Ravetz. 1991. "A New Scientific Methodology for Global Environmental Issues." In *Ecological Economics: The Science and Management of Sustainability.* Edited by Robert Costanza. New York: Columbia University Press.

Galbraith, John Kenneth. 1976. *The Affluent Society*. Third ed. New York: New American Library.

———. 1978. *The New Industrial State*. 3rd, rev. ed. New York: New American Library.

George, Jim, and David Campbell. 1990. "Patterns of Dissent and the Celebration of Difference: Critical Social Theory and International Relations." *International Studies Quarterly* 34, 3 (September):269–293.

Georgescu-Roegen, Nicholas. 1971. *The Entropy Law and the Economic Process*. Cambridge, MA: Harvard University Press.

Georgescu-Roegen, Nicholas. 1975. "Energy and Economic Myths." *Southern Economic Journal* 41, 3 (January):347–381.

Ghazi, Polly, Frank Smith, and Claire Trevena. 1995. "Fishing Fleets are Raping the Oceans." *Guardian Weekly* 152, 16 (16 April):8.

Gilbert, Alan. 1990. *Democratic Individuality*. Cambridge: Cambridge University Press.

Gilpin, Robert G. 1981. *War and Change in World Politics*. Cambridge: Cambridge University Press.

———. 1984. "The Richness of the Tradition of Political Realism." *International Organization* 38 (Spring):287–305.

Gleick, James. 1987. *Chaos: Making a New Science*. New York: Penguin Books.

Goldstein, Joshua. 1988. *Long Cycles: Prosperity and War in the Modern Age*. New Haven: Yale University Press.

Goldstein, Judith, and Robert O. Keohane. 1993. "Ideas and Foreign Policy: An Analytical Framework." In *Ideas and Foreign Policy: Beliefs, Institutions, and Political Change*. Edited by Judith Goldstein and Robert O. Keohane. Ithaca, NY: Cornell University Press.

Goodin, Robert E. 1992. *Green Political Theory*. Cambridge, UK: Polity Press, in association with Basil Blackwell.

Goodland, Robert, and Herman E. Daly. 1992. "Three Steps Towards Global Environmental Sustainability (Part I)." *Development—Journal of SID*, 2:35–41.

———. 1992. "Three Steps Towards Global Environmental Sustainability (Part II)." *Development—Journal of SID*, 3:64–71.

Goodland, Robert, Herman Daly, and John Kellenberg. 1994. "Burden Sharing in the Transition to Environmental Stability." *Futures* 26, 2 (March):146–155.

Goodwin, Neva R. 1995. "Series Introduction." In *A Survey of Ecological Economics*. Edited by Rajaram Krishnan, Jonathan M. Harris, and Neva R. Goodwin. Washington, DC: Island Press.

Gore, Vice President Al. 1992. *Earth in the Balance: Ecology and Human Spirit*. New York: Penguin Books USA.

Goulet, Denis. 1977. *The Cruel Choice: A New Concept in the Theory of Development*. New York: Atheneum.

Gray, Paul. 1996. "Bone Dry." *Time* 147, 24 (10 June):44–50.

Green, Donald P., and Ian Shapiro. 1994. *Pathologies of Rational Choice Theory: A Critique of Applications in Political Science*. New Haven: Yale University Press.

Greenwald, John. 1995. "Now He's Even Richer." *Time* 146, 8 (21 August):54–55.

Grieco, Joseph M. 1988. "Anarchy and the Limits of Cooperation: A Realist Critique of the Newest Liberal Institutionalism," *International Organization* 42, 3 (Summer):485–507.

Guimaraes, Roberto P. 1991. *The Ecopolitics of Development in the Third World: Politics and Development in Brazil.* Boulder: Lynne Rienner Publishers.

Gunder Frank, André. 1969. *Latin America: Underdevelopment or Revolution.* New York: Modern Reader.

Gunn, Alastair, and P. Aarne Vesilind. 1986. *Environmental Ethics for Engineers.* Chelsea, MI: Lewis Publishers.

Gunnell, John G. 1993. *The Descent of Political Theory: The Genealogy of an American Vocation.* Chicago: The University of Chicago Press.

Haas, Ernst B. 1980. "Why Collaborate? Issue-Linkage and International Regimes." *World Politics* 32:357–405.

———. 1983. "Words Can Hurt You: or, Who Said What to Whom About Regimes." In *International Regimes.* Edited by Stephen D. Krasner. Ithaca, NY: Cornell University Press.

Haas, Ernst B., Mary Pat Williams, and Don Babai. 1977. *Scientists and World Order: The Uses of Technical Knowledge in International Organizations.* Berkeley: University of California Press.

Haas, Peter M. 1990. *Saving the Mediterranean: The Politics of International Environmental Cooperation.* New York: Columbia University Press.

———. 1992. "Banning Chlorofluorocarbons: Epistemic Community Efforts to Protect Stratospheric Ozone." *International Organization* 46, 1 (Winter):211–235.

———. 1992. "Introduction: Epistemic Communities and International Coordination." *International Organization* 46, 1 (Winter):1–35.

Hall, Charles A. S. 1990. "Sanctioning Resource Depletion: Economic Development and Neo-Classical Economics." *The Ecologist* 20, 3 (May/June):99–104.

Hanley, Charles J. 1996. "Emptier Silos Unsettle World Food Picture." *The Denver Post* (9 November):A21.

Harcourt, G. C. 1983. "A Man for All Seasons: Talking with Kenneth Boulding." *Journal of Post Keynesian Economics* VI, 1 (Fall):143–154.

Hardin, Garrett. 1968. "The Tragedy of the Commons." *Science* 162 (13 December):1243–1248.

———. 1991. "Paramount Positions in Ecological Economics." In *Ecological Economics: The Science and Management of Sustainability.* Edited by Robert Costanza. New York: Columbia University Press.

Hardin, Russell. 1982. *Collective Action.* Baltimore: Johns Hopkins University Press.

Harrison, Neil E. 1998. "The Political Construction of Knowledge in Climate Change." Paper presented at the 38th. Annual Meeting of the International Studies Association, Minneapolis, 18–22 March.

———. 1994. "Heads in the Clouds, Feet in the Sand: Multilateral Policy Coordination in Global Environmental Issues." Ph.D. Dissertation, University of Denver, Denver, Colorado.

Harsanyi, John C. 1986. "Advances in Understanding Rational Behavior." In *Rational Choice*. Edited by Jon Elster. New York: New York University Press.

Hayek, F. A. 1994. *The Road to Serfdom*. Chicago: The University of Chicago Press, (1944).

Heilbroner, Robert L. 1980. *The Worldly Philosophers: The Lives, Times and Ideas of the Great Economic Thinkers*. 5th ed. New York: Simon and Schuster.

Hendley, Steven. 1993. "Liberalism, Communitarianism, and the Conflictual Grounds of Democratic Pluralism." *Philosophy and Social Criticism* 19, 3/4:293–316.

Hill, Christopher T. 1979. "Technological Innovation: Agent for Growth and Change." In *Technological Innovation for a Dynamic Economy*. Edited by Christopher T. Hill and James M. Utterback. Elmsford, NY: Pergamon.

Hindmarsh, Richard. 1991. "The Flawed 'Sustainable' Promise of Genetic Engineering." *The Ecologist* 21, 5 (September/October):196–205.

Hirsch, Fred. 1976. *Social Limits to Growth*. Cambridge, MA: Harvard University Press.

Hodgson, Geoffrey M. 1994. "The Evolution of Socioeconomic Order in the Move to a Market Economy." *Review of International Political Economy* 1, 3 (Autumn):387–404.

Hoeller, Peter, Andrew Dean, and Jon Nicolaisen. 1990. "A Survey of the Costs of Reducing Greenhouse Gas Emissions." OECD Working Paper No. 89, Department of Economics and Statistics. Paris: Organization for Economic Cooperation and Development, 1990.

Hoffman, John. 1984. *The Gramscian Challenge: Coercion and Consent in Marxist Political Theory*. New York: Basil Blackwell.

Holland, John H. 1995. *Hidden Order: How Adaptation Builds Complexity*. Reading, MA: Perseus Books.

Holsti, K. J. 1986. "The Horsemen of the Apocalypse: At the Gate, Detoured, or Retreating?" *International Studies Quarterly* 30 :355–372.

Houghton, John. 1994. *Global Warming: The Complete Briefing*. Oxford: Lion Publishing.

Houghton, J. T., B. A. Callander, and S. K. Varney, eds. 1992. *Climate Change 1992: The Supplementary Report to the IPCC Scientific Assessment*. Cambridge: Cambridge University Press, for the Intergovernmental Panel on Climate Change.

"How Do You Mean, Fair?" *The Economist* 327, 7813 (29 May, 1993):71.

"How Does Your Economy Grow?" *The Economist* 336, 7934 (30 September, 1995):96.

"How Not to Catch Up" *The Economist* 326, 7793 (9 January, 1993):19–21.

"How to Mine a Flying Mountain" *The Economist* 333, 7895 (24 December, 1994): 97–98.

Idso, Sherwood B. 1989. *Carbon Dioxide and Global Change: Earth in Transition*. Tempe, AZ: IBR Press.

Iida, Keisuke. 1993. "Analytic Uncertainty and International Cooperation: Theory and Application to International Economic Policy Coordination." *International Studies Quarterly* 37, 4 (December):431–457.

Inglehart, Ronald. 1990. *Culture Shift in Advanced Industrial Society.* Princeton: Princeton University Press.

Intergovernmental Panel on Climate Change (1990a). "IPCC First Assessment Report, Volume 1: Overview." August 1990.

———. 1990b. "IPCC First Assessment Report, Volume 1." August 1990.

———. 1995. "IPCC Second Assessment: Climate Change 1995." A Report of the Intergovernmental Panel on Climate Change.

Jervis, Robert. 1997. *System Effects: Complexity in Political and Social Life.* Princeton: Princeton University Press.

Johnson, Chalmers. 1982. *MITI and the Japanese Miracle.* Stanford: Stanford University Press.

Kammen, Michael G. 1966. "Virginia at the Close of the Seventeenth Century: An Appraisal by James Blair and John Locke." *Virginia Magazine of History and Biography* 74 (April):141–169.

Kateb, George. 1989. "Individualism, Communitarianism, and Docility." *Social Research* 56, 4 (Winter):921–942.

Kates, Robert W. 1994. "Sustaining Life on Earth." *Scientific American* 271, 4 (October 1994):114–122.

Kauffman, Stuart. 1995. *At Home in the Universe: The Search for the Laws of Self-Organization and Complexity.* New York: Oxford University Press.

Keeney, Ralph L. 1992. *Value-Focused Thinking.* Cambridge, MA: Harvard University Press.

Keillor, Garrison. 1995. "Minnesota's Sensible Plan." *Time* 146 (11 September):84–85.

Keohane, Robert O. 1983. "The Demand for International Regimes." In *International Regimes.* Edited by Stephen D. Krasner. Ithaca, NY: Cornell University Press.

———. 1984. *After Hegemony: Cooperation and Discord in the World Economy.* Princeton: Princeton University Press.

———. 1985. "Reciprocity in International Relations." *International Organization* 40 (Winter):1–27.

———. 1988. "International Institutions: Two Approaches." *International Studies Quarterly* 32, 4 (December):379–396.

———. 1989. *International Institutions and State Power: Essays in International Relations Theory.* Boulder, CO: Westview Press.

Keohane, Robert O., and Robert Axelrod. 1986. "Achieving Cooperation Under Anarchy: Strategies and Institutions." In *Cooperation Under Anarchy.* Edited by Kenneth A. Oye. Princeton: Princeton University Press.

Keohane, Robert O., Peter M. Haas, and Marc A. Levy. 1993. "The Effectiveness of International Environmental Institutions." In *Institutions for the Earth: Sources of Effective International Environmental Protection.* Edited by Peter M. Haas, Robert O. Keohane, and Marc A. Levy. Cambridge, MA: MIT Press.

Keohane, Robert O. and Joseph S. Nye, eds. 1971. *Transnational Relations and World Politics.* Cambridge, MA: Harvard University Press.

———. 1989. *Power and Interdependence.* 2nd ed. Boston: Little, Brown.

Keyfitz, Nathan. 1995. "Inter-disciplinary Contradictions and the Influence of Science on Policy." *Policy Sciences* 28, 1:21–38.

Kindleberger, Charles P. 1981. "Dominance and Leadership in the International Economy." *International Studies Quarterly* 25, 2:242–54.

Kingdon, John W. 1984. *Agendas, Alternatives, and Public Policies.* Boston: Little, Brown.

Kraft, Michael E., and Norman J. Vig. 1990. "Environmental Policy from the Seventies to the Nineties: Continuity and Change." In *Environmental Policy in the 1990s.* Edited by Norman J. Vig and Michael E. Kraft. Washington, DC: CQ Press.

Krasner, Stephen D. 1978. *Defending the National Interest, Raw Material Investments and US Foreign Policy.* Princeton: Princeton University Press.

———. 1983. "Structural Causes and Regime Consequences: Regimes as Intervening Variables." In: *International Regimes.* Edited by Stephen D. Krasner. Ithaca, NY: Cornell University Press.

Krugman, Paul. 1994. "The Myth of Asia's Miracle." *Foreign Affairs* 73, 6 (November/December):62–78.

Kubalkova,Vendulka, Nicholas Onuf, and Paul Kowert, eds. 1998. *International Relations in a Constructed World.* Armonk, NY: M.E. Sharpe.

Kuhn, Thomas. 1970. *The Structure of Scientific Revolutions.* 2nd ed. Chicago: University of Chicago Press.

Kymlicka, Will. 1989. *Liberalism, Community and Culture.* Oxford: Clarendon Press.

———. 1990. *Contemporary Political Philosophy: An Introduction.* Oxford: Clarendon Press.

Larson, David A., and Walton T. Wilford. 1979. "The Physical Quality of Life Index: A Useful Social Indicator?" *World Development* 7, 6 (June 1979):581–584.

"The Lawnmower's Tale." *The Economist* 334, 7905 (11 March, 1995):79–82.

Lederman, Leonard L. 1994. "A Comparative Analysis of Civilian Technology Strategies Among Some Nations: France, the Federal Republic of Germany, Japan, the United Kingdom, and the United States." *Policy Studies Journal* 22, 2:279–295.

Lélé, Sharachchandra M. 1991. "Sustainable Development: A Critical Review." *World Development* 19, 6:607–621.

Lemonick, Michael D. 1997. "Turning Down the Heat." *Time* 150, no. 26 (22 December):23–27.

Leopold, Aldo. 1970. *A Sand County Almanac.* New York: Ballantine Books.

Lester, James P., ed. 1989. *Environmental Politics and Policy: Theories and Evidence.* Durham: Duke University Press.

Levine, David. 1988. *Needs, Rights, and the Market.* Boulder: Lynne Rienner Publishers.

Levine, David P. 1995. *Wealth and Freedom: An Introduction to Political Economy.* Cambridge: Cambridge University Press.

Levy, Marc A. 1993. "European Acid Rain: The Power of Tote Board Diplomacy." In *Institutions for the Earth: Sources of Effective International Environmental Protection.* Edited by Peter M. Haas, Robert O. Keohane, and Marc A. Levy. Cambridge, MA: MIT Press.

Levy, Marc A., Robert O. Keohane, and Peter M. Haas. 1993. "Improving the Effectiveness of International Environmental Institutions." In *Institutions for the Earth: Sources of Effective International Environmental Protection.* Edited by Peter M. Haas, Robert O. Keohane, and Marc A. Levy. Cambridge, MA: MIT Press.

Lewis, W. Arthur. 1955. *The Theory of Economic Growth.* Homewood, IL: Richard D. Irwin.

Limbaugh, Rush H., III. 1993. *See, I Told You So.* New York: Pocket Books.

Lindblom, Charles E. 1959. "The Science of Muddling Through." *Public Administration Review* 14 (Spring):79–88.

———. 1980. *The Policy-Making Process.* Englewood Cliffs, NJ: Prentice Hall.

———. 1977. *Politics and Markets.* New York: Basic Books.

Lipsey, Richard G., Peter O. Steiner, and Douglas D. Purvis. 1984. *Economics.* 7th ed. New York: Harper & Row.

Lipsher, Steve. 1995. "Glacial Melting Points to Warming, Studies Show." *The Denver Post* (9 July):A12.

Litfin, Karen T. 1994. *Ozone Discourses: Science and Politics in Global Environmental Cooperation.* New York: Columbia University Press.

Locke, John. 1980. *Second Treatise of Government.* Indianapolis: Hackett.

Lovins, Amory B. 1976. "Energy Strategy: The Road Not Taken?" *Foreign Affairs* 55, 1 (October):65–96.

Lowi, Miriam R. 1993. "Bridging the Divide: Transboundary Resource Disputes and the Case of West Bank Water." *International Security* 18, 1 (Summer):113–138.

Luce, R. Duncan, and Howard Raiffa. 1957. *Games and Decisions: Introduction and Critical Survey.* New York: Wiley.

Luke, Timothy W. 1994. "Sustaining the Earth or Maintaining the Economy? The Contradictions of Sustainable Development." Paper presented at the Annual Meeting of the American Political Science Association, August 30–September 4, 1994.

MacIntyre, Alasdair. 1988. *Whose Justice? Which Rationality?* Notre Dame, Indiana: University of Notre Dame Press.

Manes, Christopher. 1990. *Green Rage.* Boston: Little, Brown.

Mansfield, Edwin. 1968. *The Economics of Technological Change.* New York: W. W. Norton.

———. 1982. "Tax Policy and Innovation." *Science* 215:1365–1371.

———. 1991. "Academic Research and Industrial Innovation." *Research Policy* 20, 1 (January):1–12.

———. 1991. "Social Returns from R&D: Findings, Methods and Limitations." *Research Technology Management* 34, 6 (1 November):24–27.

Mapel, David R. 1990. "Prudence and the Plurality of Value in International Ethics." *Journal of Politics* 52, 2 (May):433–456.

Martin, Lisa L. 1993. "The Rational State Choice of Multilateralism." In *Multilateralism Matters: The Theory and Praxis of an Institutional Form.* Edited by John Gerard Ruggie. New York: Columbia University Press.

Martin, Michael C. J. 1994. *Managing Innovation and Entrepreneurship in Technology-Based Firms*. New York: J. Wiley.

McCormick, James M. 1992. *American Foreign Policy and Process*. 2nd ed. Itasca, IL: F. E. Peacock Publishers.

McCormick, John. 1989. *Reclaiming Paradise: The Global Environmental Movement*. Bloomington: Indiana University Press.

McLean, Iain. 1991. "Rational Choice and Politics." *Political Studies* 39:496–512.

McLean, Ian. 1987. *Public Choice: An Introduction*. Oxford: Basil Blackwell.

Meadows, Dennis L., and Jorgen Randers. "Adding the Time Dimension to Environmental Policy." In *World Eco-Crisis*. Edited by David Kay and Eugene Skolnikoff. Madison,WI: University of Wisconsin Press.

Meadows, Donella H., Dennis L. Meadows, Jorgen Randers, and William W. Behrens, III. 1972. *The Limits to Growth*. New York: Universe Books.

Michaels, Patrick J. 1992. *Sound and Fury: The Science and Politics of Global Warming*. Washington, DC: The Cato Institute.

"Microsoft's Web of Fear." *The Economist* 326, 7793 (9 January, 1993):58–60.

Milbrath, Lester W. 1989. *Envisioning a Sustainable Society: Learning Our Way Out*. Albany: State University of New York Press, Albany.

———. 1984. *Environmentalists: Vanguard for a New Society*. Albany: State University of New York Press.

Mill, John Stuart. 1974 [1859]. *On Liberty*. Harmondsworth: Penguin Books.

———. 1957. *Utilitarianism*. Edited by Oskar Piest. Indianapolis: Bobbs-Merrill.

Miller, Ed L. 1993. *Questions that Matter: An Invitation to Philosophy*. Shorter ed. New York: McGraw-Hill.

Miller, Marian A. L. 1995. *The Third World in Global Environmental Politics*. Boulder: Lynne Rienner.

Mills, C. Wright. 1956. *The Power Elite*. New York: Oxford University Press.

Molina, Mario J., and F. Sherwood Rowland. 1974. "Stratospheric Sink for Chorofluoromethanes: Chlorine Atomic Catalysed Destruction of Ozone." *Nature* 249:810–12.

Moon, J. Donald. 1993. "Pluralism and Progress in the Study of Politics." In *The Theory and Practice of Political Science*. Edited by William Crotty. Evanston: Northwestern University Press.

Moore, Curtis, and Alan Miller. 1994. *Green Gold: Japan, Germany, the United States, and the Race for Environmental Technology*. Boston: Beacon Press.

Morgenthau, Hans J. 1978. *Politics Among Nations: The Struggle for Peace and Power*. 5th ed., rev. New York: Alfred A. Knopf.

Morrice, David. 1994. "C. B. Macpherson's Critque of Liberal Democracy and Capitalism." *Political Studies* 42, 4 (December):646–661.

Morrisette, Peter M. 1989. "The Evolution of Policy Responses to Stratospheric Ozone Depletion." *Natural Resources Journal* 29 (Summer):793–820.

Mowery, David, and Nathan Rosenberg. 1979. "The Influence of Market Demand Upon Innovation: A Critical Review of Some Recent Empirical Studies." *Research Policy* 8, 2 (February):102–153.

Mueller, Dennis C. 1989. *Public Choice II*. Cambridge: Cambridge University Press.

Naess, Arne. 1985. "Identification as a Source of Deep Ecological Attitudes." In *Deep Ecology*. Edited by Michael Tobias. San Diego: Avant Books.

———. 1995. "The Deep Ecological Movement: Some Philosophical Aspects." In *Deep Ecology for the 21st Century*. Edited by George Sessions. Boston: Shambhala.

Nanda, Ved P. 1995. "Crisis Heats Up Over Global Fish Stocks." *The Denver Post* (16 April):D4.

Nardin, Terry. 1992. "Ethics Traditions in International Affairs." In *Traditions of International Ethics*. Edited by Terry Nardin and David R. Mapel. Cambridge: Cambridge University Press.

National Commission on the Environment. 1993. *Choosing a Sustainable Development: The Report of the National Commission on the Environment*. Washington, D.C.: Island Press.

National Research Council. 1979. *Protection Against Depletion of Stratospheric Ozone by Chlorofluorocarbons*. Washington, DC: National Academy of Sciences.

Nelson, Richard R. 1990. "Capitalism as an Engine of Progress." *Research Policy* 19, 3 (May):193–214.

———. 1995. "Recent Theorizing About Economic Change." *Journal of Economic Literature* XXXIII (March):48–90.

Nelson, Richard R. and Sidney G. Winter. 1982. *An Evolutionary Theory of Economic Change*. Cambridge, MA: Harvard University Press.

Nelson, Richard R., Sidney G. Winter, and H. Schuette. 1976. "Technical Change in an Evolutionary Model." *Quarterly Journal of Economics* 40:90–118.

Noble, David F. 1984. *Forces of Production: A Social History of Industrial Automation*. New York: Knopf.

Nordhaus, William J. 1990. "Count Before You Leap." *The Economist* 316, 7662 (7 July):21–24.

Nozick, Robert. 1974. *Anarchy, State, and Utopia*. New York: Basic Books.

———. 1993. *The Nature of Rationality*. Princeton: Princeton University Press.

Nye, Joseph S., Jr. 1990. *Bound to Lead: The Changing Nature of American Power*. New York: Basic Books.

O'Connor, Martin, ed. 1994. *Is Capitalism Sustainable?: Political Economy and the Politics of Ecology*. New York: The Guildford Press.

Odum, Eugene P. 1993. *Ecology and Our Endangered Life-Support Systems*. 2nd ed. Sunderland, MA: Sinauer Associates.

OECD/IEA (1993). *World Energy Outlook to the Year 2010*. Paris: International Energy Agency and OECD.

Okun, Arthur M. 1975. *Equality and Efficiency: The Big Tradeoff*. Washington, DC: The Brookings Institution.

Olson, Mancur. 1982. *The Rise and Decline Of Nations : Economic Growth, Stagflation, and Social Rigidities*. New Haven: Yale University Press.

———. 1965. *The Logic of Collective Action: Public Goods and the Theory of Groups*. Cambridge, MA: Harvard University Press.

Onuf, Nicholas Greenwood. 1989. *World of Our Making: Rules and Rule in Social Theory and International Relations*. Columbia, SC: University of South Carolina Press.

Ophuls, William, and Stephan A. Boyan, Jr. 1992. *Ecology and the Politics of Scarcity Revisited.* New York: W. H. Freeman.

Orr, David W. 1992. "Pascal's Wager and Economics in a Hotter Time." *The Ecologist* 22, 2 (March/April):42–43.

Oshima, K. 1984. "Technological Innovation and Industrial Research in Japan." *Research Policy* 13, 6 (December):287–301.

Ostrom, Elinor. 1990. *Governing the Commons: The Evolution of Institutions for Collective Action.* Cambridge, MA: Cambridge University Press.

———. 1999. "Coping with Tragedies of the Commons." *Annual Review of Political Science* 2: forthcoming.

Ostrom, Elinor, Roy Gardner, and James Walker. 1994. *Rules, Games, and Common-Pool Resources.* Ann Arbor: The University of Michigan Press.

Pacey, Arnold. 1983. *The Culture of Technology.* Cambridge, MA: MIT Press.

Paehlke, Robert C. 1989. *Environmentalism and the Future of Progressive Politics.* New Haven: Yale University Press.

Page, Jake. "Ranchers Form a 'Radical Center' to Protect Wide-open Spaces." *Smithsonian* 28, 3 (1997):50–61.

Palma, Gabriel. 1978. "Dependency: A Formal Theory of Underdevelopment for the Analysis of Concrete Situations of Underdevelopment." *World Development* 6:881–924.

Parry, Martin. 1990. *Climate Change and World Agriculture.* London: Earthscan Publications, in association with The International Institute for Applied Systems Science and the United Nations Environment Programme.

Pearce, David. 1989. "An Economic Perspective on Sustainable Development." *Development—Journal of SID,* 2/3:17–19.

Pearce, David, Edward Barbier, and Anil Markandya. 1990. *Sustainable Development: Economics and Environment in the Third World.* Aldershot: Edward Elgar Publishing.

Pearce, David, Anil Markandya, and Edward B. Barbier. 1989. *Blueprint for a Green Economy.* London: Earthscan Publications.

Pearce, David W., and R. Kerry Turner. 1990. *Economics of Natural Resources and the Environment.* Baltimore: The Johns Hopkins University Press.

Pellicani, Luciano. 1981. *Gramsci: An Alternative Communism?* Stanford: Hoover Institution Press.

Petracca, Mark P. 1991. "The Rational Choice Approach to Politics: A Challenge to Democratic Theory." *The Review of Politics* 53 (Spring):289–319.

Pirsig, Robert M. 1974. *Zen and the Art of Motorcycle Maintenance: An Inquiry into Values.* New York: Morrow Quill Paperbacks.

"Plant Workers." *The Economist* 335, 7913 (6 May, 1995):79–80.

Plumwood, Val. 1992. "Feminism and Ecofeminism: Beyond the Dualistic Assumptions of Women, Men and Nature." *The Ecologist* 22, 1 (January/February):8–13.

Polanyi, Karl. 1944. *The Great Transformation.* Boston: Beacon.

———. 1971. "Aristotle Discovers the Economy." In *Trade and Market in the Early Empires.* Edited by Karl Polanyi, Conrad M. Arensberg, and Harry W. Pearson. Chicago, IL: Henry Regnery.

"Policing Thoughts." *The Economist* 324, 7773 (22 August, 1992):55–56.

"The Politics of Restoration." *The Economist* 333, 7895 (December, 1994):33–36.

"Pollock Overboard." *The Economist* 338, 7947 (6 January, 1995):21–22.

Polsby, Nelson W. 1984. *Political Innovation in America: The Politics of Policy Initiation.* New Haven: Yale University Press.

Ponte, Lowell. 1976. *The Cooling.* Englewood Cliffs, NJ: Prentice Hall.

Pooley, Eric. "Cows or Condos? Putting Aside their Differences, Conservative Cattlemen and Left-Leaning Environmentalists Team up to Save a Valley." *Time.* 150, 1 (7 July, 1997):78–84.

"The Poor and the Rich." *The Economist* 339, 7967 (25 May, 1996):23–25.

Porter, Gareth, and Janet Welsh Brown. 1991. *Global Environmental Politics.* Boulder: Westview Press.

Powell, Robert. 1994. "Anarchy in International Relations Theory: The Neorealist-Neoliberal Debate." *International Organization* 48, 2 (Spring):313–344.

"The Price of Imagining Arden." *The Economist* 333, 7892 (3 December, 1994):80.

"The Price of Light." *The Economist* 333, 7886 (22 October, 1994):84.

Price, Derek deS. 1983. "The Science/Technology Relationship, the Craft of Experimental Science, and Policy for the Improvement of High Technology Innovation." *Research Policy* 13:3–20.

Prigogine, Ilya, and Isabelle Stengers. 1984. *Order Out of Chaos: Man's New Dialogue with Nature.* New York: New American Library.

Princen, Thomas; Matthias Finger. 1994. *Environmental NGOs in World Politics: Linking the Local and the Global.* London: Routledge.

Putnam, Robert D. 1988. "Diplomacy and Domestic Politics: the Logic of Two-Level Games." *International Organization* 42 (Summer):427–460.

———. 1993. *Making Democracy Work: Civic Traditions in Modern Italy.* Princeton: Princeton University Press.

Rachels, James. 1986. *The Elements of Moral Philosophy.* New York: McGraw-Hill.

"Rational Economic Man: The Human Factor." *The Economist* 333, 7895 (24 December, 1994):90–92.

Raval, A. and V. Ramanathan. 1989. "Observational Determination of the Greenhouse Effect." *Nature* 342, 6251:758–761.

Rawls, John.1971. *A Theory of Justice.* Cambridge, MA: The Belknap Press of Harvard University Press.

Ray, Dixie Lee, and Lou Guzzo. 1994. *Environmental Overkill: Whatever Happened to Common Sense?* New York: Harper Perennial.

"Reading the Patterns." *The Economist* 335, 7908 (1 April, 1995):65–67.

Rees, William E. 1990. "The Ecology of Sustainable Development." *The Ecologist* 20, 1 (Jan/Feb):18–23.

Regan, Tom. 1983. *The Case for Animals Rights.* Berkeley: University of California Press.

Rennie, John. 1995. "The Uncertainties of Technological Innovation." *Scientific American* 273, 3 (September):57–58.

Repetto, Robert. 1992. "Environmental Taxes and U.S. Competitiveness." *Columbia Journal of World Business,* Fall & Winter:128–134.

Revelle, R. and H. E. Suess 1957. "Carbon Dioxide Exchange Between Atmosphere and Ocean and the Question of an Increase of Atmospheric $CO_2$ During Past and Present Decades." *Tellus* 9 (Jan):18–27.

Reynolds, Morgan O. 1985. *Crime by Choice: An Economic Analysis*. Dallas: Fisher Institute.

Ritchie, Mark. 1992. "Free Trade versus Sustainable Agriculture: The Implications of NAFTA." *The Ecologist* 22, 5 (September/October):221–227.

Roe, Emery. 1994. *Narrative Policy Analysis: Theory and Practice*. Durham: Duke University Press.

Rolston, Holmes, III. 1988. *Environmental Ethics: Duties to and Values in The Natural World*. Philadelphia: Temple University Press.

———. 1994. "Value in Nature and the Nature of Value." In *Philosophy and the Natural Environment*. Edited by Robin Attfield and Andrew Belsey. Cambridge: Cambridge University Press.

Romer, Paul. 1986. "Increasing Returns and Long Run Growth." *Journal of Political Economy* 94, 5:1002–35.

Rosenau, James N. 1990. *Turbulence in World Politics: A Theory of Change and Continuity*. Princeton: Princeton University Press.

Rosenberg, Nathan. 1982. *Inside the Black Box: Technology and Economics*. Cambridge: Cambridge University Press.

———. 1994. "How the Developed Countries Became Rich." *Daedalus* 123, 4 (Fall):127–140.

———. 1995. "Why Technology Forecasts Fail." *The Futurist* 29, 4 (1 July):16–21.

Rosenberg, Nathan, and L. E. Birdzell Jr. 1990. "Science, Technology and the Western Miracle." *Scientific American* 263, 5 (November):42–54.

Rothschild, Kurt W. 1993. *Ethics and Economic Theory: Ideas-Models-Dilemmas*. Aldershot, UK: Edward Elgar.

Rothwell, Roy, and Mark Dodgson. 1992. "European Technology Policy Evolution: Convergence Towards SMEs and Regional Technology Transfer." *Technovation* 12, 4:223–238.

Rothwell, Roy, and Walter Zegveld. 1985. *Reindustrialization and Technology*. Harlow: Longman.

Ruggie, John Gerard. 1983. "International Regimes, Transactions, and Change: Embedded Liberalism in the Postwar Economic Order." In *International Regimes*. Edited by Stephen D. Krasner. Ithaca, NY: Cornell University Press.

Rumelt, Richard P., Dan E. Schendel, and David J. Teece, eds. 1994. *Fundamental Issues in Strategy: A Research Agenda*. Boston, MA: Harvard Business School Press.

———. 1992. "Multilateralism: the Anatomy of an Institution." *International Organization* 46, 3 (Summer):561–598.

———, ed. 1993. *Multilateralism Matters: The Theory and Praxis of an Institutional Form*. New York: Columbia University Press.

Sachs, Wolfgang. 1990. "On the Archaeology of the Development Idea." *The Ecologist* 20, 2 (March/April):42–43.

Saetevik, Sunneva. 1988. *Environmental Cooperation between the North Sea States*. London: Belhaven Press.

Sagoff, Mark. 1988. *The Economy of the Earth*. New York: Cambridge University Press.

———. 1988. "Some Problems with Environmental Economics." *Environmental Ethics* 10, 1 (Spring):55–74.

Sahal, Devendra. 1981. *Patterns of Technological Innovation*. Reading, MA: Addison-Wesley.

Sale, Kirkpatrick. 1980. *Human Scale*. New York: Coward, McCann & Geoghegan.

Salter, W. 1960. *Productivity and Technical Change*. Cambridge: Cambridge University Press.

Sarkar, Saral. 1990. "Accommodating Industrialism: A Third World View of the West German Ecological Movement." *The Ecologist* 20, 4 (July/August):147–152.

Schiesser, Walter. 1992. "The Rocky Road to Sustainable Development." *Swiss Review of World Affairs* (July):6–8.

Schmandt, J. 1981. "Toward a Theory of the Modern State." In *Technology and International Affairs*. Edited by Joseph Szyliswicz. New York: Praeger, 1981.

Schlossberger, Eugene. 1993. *The Ethical Engineer*. Philadelphia: Temple University Press.

Schmookler, Andrew Bard. 1993. *Fool's Gold: The Fate of Values in a World of Goods*. San Francisco: Harper San Francisco.

Schmookler, J. 1966. *Inventions and Economic Growth*. Cambridge, MA: Harvard University Press.

Schneider, Stephen H. 1977. *The Genesis Strategy: Climate and Global Survival*. New York: Dell Publishing.

———. 1989. *Global Warming: Are We Entering the Greenhouse Century?* New York: Vintage Books.

———. 1990. "The Global Warming Debate: Science or Politics?" *Environmental Science and Technology* 24 (Apr):432–435.

Schumacher, E. F. 1974. *Small is Beautiful: A Study of Economics as if People Mattered*. London: Sphere Books.

Schumpeter, Joseph A. 1934. *The Theory of Economic Development*. Cambridge, MA: Harvard University Press.

———. 1954. *History of Economic Analysis*. New York: Oxford University Press.

———. 1961. *Capitalism, Socialism and Democracy*. London: George Allen and Unwin.

Schwarzenbach, Sibyl. 1988. "Locke's Two Conceptions of Property." *Social Theory and Practice* 14, 2 (Summer):141–172.

Schweitzer, Albert. 1946. *Civilization and Ethics*. London: A. & C. Black.

Scitovsky, Tibor. 1976. *The Joyless Economy: An Inquiry into Human Satisfaction and Consumer Dissatisfaction*. New York: Oxford University Press.

Sessions, George. 1995. "Deep Ecology and the New Age Movement." In *Deep Ecology for the 21st. Century*, edited by George Sessions. Boston: Shambhala.

Shackley, Simon, and Brian Wynne. 1995. "Global Climate Change: Mutual Construction of an Emergent Science-Policy Domain." *Science and Public Policy* 22, no. 4 (August):218–230.

———. 1996. "Representing Uncertainty in Global Climate Change Science and Policy: Boundary Ordering Devices and Authority." *Science, Technology, & Human Values* 21, no. 3 (Summer):275–302.

Simon, Herbert A. 1972. "Theories of Bounded Rationality." In *Decision and Organization*. Edited by C. B. Radner and R. Radner. Amsterdam: North-Holland.

Singer, Peter. 1985. *In Defense of Animals*. New York: Basil Blackwell.

Singer, S. Fred. 1984. "World Demand for Oil." In *The Resourceful Earth: A Response to Global 2000*. Edited by Julian Simon and Herman Kahn. New York: Basil Blackwell.

———. 1992. "Sustainable Development vs. Global Environment: Resolving the Conflict." *Columbia Journal of World Business*, Fall & Winter:154–162.

Sitarz, Daniel, ed. 1993. *Agenda 21: The Earth Summit Strategy to Save Our Planet*. Boulder, CO: Earth Press.

Smith, Adam. 1776. *An Inquiry Into the Nature and Causes of the Wealth of Nations*. Vols. 1 and 2. Indianapolis: Liberty Classics.

———. 1976. *The Theory of Moral Sentiments*. Edited by D.D. Raphael and A.L. Macfie. Oxford: Clarendon Press.

Smith, Merritt Roe. 1985. *Military Enterprises and Technological Change*. Cambridge, MA: MIT Press.

Smith, Steve, Ken Booth, and Marysia Zalewski, eds. 1996. *International Theory: Positivism & Beyond*. Cambridge: Cambridge University Press.

Snidal, Duncan. 1991. "Relative Gains and the Pattern of International Cooperation." *American Political Science Review* 85 (September):701–26.

———. 1985. "Coordination Versus Prisoner's Dilemma: Implications for International Cooperation and Regimes." *American Political Science Review* 79 (December):923–47.

Solow, Robert M. 1957. "Technical Progress and Productivity Change." *Review of Economics and Statistics* 39:312–320.

———. 1993. "Sustainability: An Economist's Perspective." In *Economics of the Environment: Selected Readings*. 3rd. ed. Edited by Robert Dorfman and Nancy Dorfman. New York: W. W. Norton.

"Some Day. . . ." *The Economist* 333, 7893 (10 December, 1994):90–91.

Speth, James Gustave. 1989. "The Environment: The Greening of Technology." *Development—Journal of SID* 2/3:30–36.

Sprinz, Detlef, and Tapani Vaahtoranta. 1994. "The Interest-Based Explanation of International Environmental Policy." *International Organization* 48, 1 (Winter):77–106.

"Squeezed: A Survey of the Arab World." *The Economist* 315, 7654 (12 May, 1990):9–12.

"Stay Cool." *The Economist* 335, 7906 (1 April, 1995):11–12.

Stever, James A. 1995. "After All This, Here Come the Conservatives." *Public Administration Review* 55:486–490.

Stewart, Frances. 1985. *Planning to Meet Basic Needs*. London: Macmillan.

Stewart, Frances, and Paul Streeten. 1971. "Conflicts Between Output and Employment Objectives in Developing Countries." *Oxford Economic Papers* 20 (July):145–168.

———. 1976. "New Strategies for Development: Poverty, Income Distribution, and Growth." *Oxford Economic Papers* 28 (November):381–405.

Stirling, Andrew. 1993. "Environmental Valuation: How Much is the Emperor Wearing?" *The Ecologist* 23, 3 (May/June):97–103.

Stone, Christopher D. 1974. *Should Trees Have Standing.* Los Altos, CA: William Kaufman.

———. 1993. *The Gnat is Older than Man: Global Environment and Human Agenda.* Princeton: Princeton University Press.

Stone, Deborah A. 1988. *Policy Paradox and Political Reason.* Glenview, IL: Scott, Foresman and Company.

Taylor, Bob Pepperman. 1992. *Our Limits Transgressed: Environmental Political Thought in America.* Lawrence, KS: University Press of Kansas.

Taylor, Paul. 1986. *Respect for Nature: A Theory of Environmental Ethics.* Princeton: Princeton University Press.

Taylor, Philip. 1984. *Nonstate Actors in International Politics: From Transregional to Substate Organizations.* Boulder and London: Westview Press.

Tegart, W. J. McG., and G. W. Sheldon, eds. 1993. *Climate Change 1992: The Supplementary Report to the IPCC Impacts Assessment.* Canberra: Australian Government Publishing Service.

"The Cost of Keeping Cool." *The Economist* 318, 7691 (4 May, 1991):59.

"The Left Rises from the Almost-Dead." *The Economist* 344, no. 8033 (6 September 1997):25–27.

Thomas, Lewis. 1975. *The Lives of a Cell.* New York: Bantam Books.

Thurow, Lester C. 1986. "The Economic Case Against Star Wars." *Technology Review* 89, 2 (February/March):11–15.

Tidd, Joseph, John Bessant, and Keith Pavitt. 1997. *Managing Innovation: Integration Technological and Organizational Change.* New York: J. Wiley.

Tietenberg, Tom. 1994. *Environmental Economics and Policy.* New York: Harper Collins College Publishers.

Titus, James G., ed. 1986. *Effects of Changes on Stratospheric Ozone and Global Climate.* Washington DC: United States Environmental Protection Agency.

Toulmin, Stephen. 1982. *The Return to Cosmology: Postmodern Science and the Theology of Nature.* Berkeley: University of California Press.

United States, Department of Energy. 1991. *National Energy Strategy: Powerful Ideas for America*, First 1991/1992 ed. Washington, DC: Government Printing Office.

van den Bergh, C. J. M. Jeroen, and Jan van der Straaten. 1994. *Toward Sustainable Development: Concepts, Methods, and Policy.* Washington, DC: Island Press for the International Society for Ecological Economics.

Vasquez, John A. 1983. *The Power of Power Politics: a Critique.* New Brunswick, New Jersey: Rutgers University Press.

Verweij, Marco. 1995. "Cultural Theory and the Study of International Relations." *Millennium: Journal of International Studies* 24, 1:87–111.

Vickers, Douglas. 1994. *Economics and the Antagonism of Time: Time, Uncertainty, and Choice in Economic Theory.* Ann Arbor: The University of Michigan Press.

Vig, Norman J. and Michael E. Kraft, eds. 1990. *Environmental Policy in the 1990s.* Washington, DC: Congressional Quarterly Inc.

Vitousek, Peter M., et al. 1986. "Human Appropriation of the Products of Photosynthesis." *Bioscience* 34, 6:368–373.

Waldrop, M. Mitchell. 1992. *Complexity: the Emerging Science at the Edge of Order and Chaos.* New York: Simon & Schuster.

Wallerstein, Immanuel. 1979. *The Capitalist World Economy.* Cambridge: Cambridge University Press.

Waltz, Kenneth. 1979. *Theory of International Politics.* Reading MA: Addison-Wesley.

Wapner, Paul. 1996. *Environmental Activism and World Civic Politics.* Albany: State University of New York Press.

Ward, Hugh. 1992. "Game Theory and the Politics of the Global Commons." *Journal of Conflict Resolution* 37, 2:203–35.

"War of the Worlds: A Survey of the Global Economy." *The Economist* 333, 7883 (1 October, 1994).

Warren, Karen J. 1990. "The Power and the Promise of Ecological Feminism." *Environmental Ethics* 12 (Summer):125–145.

Watson, R. T., L. G. Meiro Filho, E. Sanhueza, and A. Janetos (1992). "Greenhouse Gases: Sources and Sinks." In *Climate Change 1992: The Supplementary Report to the IPCC Scientific Assessment.* Edited by J. T. Houghton, B. A. Callendar, and S. K. Varney. Cambridge: Cambridge University Press, for the Intergovernmental Panel on Climate Change.

Watson, R.T. and Ozone Trends Panel, M. J. Prather and Ad Hoc Theory Panel, and Michael J. Kurylo and NASA Panel for Data Evaluation. 1988. *Present State Of Knowledge of the Upper Atmosphere 1988: An Assessment Report.* Washington, DC: U.S. Government Printing Office.

Webb, Michael C., and Stephen D. Krasner. 1989. "Hegemonic Stability Theory: An Empirical Assessment." *Review of International Studies* 15:193–198.

Webre, Philip, and David Bodde. 1986. "High Technology's Stake in Tax Reform." *Technology Review* 87, 5 (July):26–34.

Weinberg, Alvin M. 1986. "Can Technology Replace Social Engineering?" In *Technology and the Future.* 4th ed. Edited by Albert H. Teich. New York: St. Martin's Press.

Wells, Louis T., Jr. 1984. "Economic Man and Engineering Man." In *Technology Crossing Borders.* Edited by Robert Stobaugh and Louis T. Wells, Jr. Boston: Harvard Business School Press.

Wendt, Alexander E. 1987. "The Agent-Structure Problem in International Relations Theory." *International Organization* 41, 3 (Summer):337–370.

———. 1992. "Anarchy is What States Make of it: The Social Construction of Power Politics." *International Organization* 6 (Spring):391–425.

"When the State Picks Winners." *The Economist* 326, 7793 (9 January, 1993):13–14.

White, Lawrence J. 1985. "Clearing the Legal Path to Cooperative Research." *Technology Review* 88, 5 (July):38–44.

White, Robert H. 1990. "The Great Climate Debate." *Scientific American* 263 (July):41.

Wildavsky, Aaron. 1979. *Speaking Truth to Power*. Boston: Little, Brown.

"Will the World Starve?" *The Economist* 335, 7918 (10 June, 1995):39–40.

Wilson, Robert W., et al. 1980. *Innovation Competition, and Government Policy in the Semiconductor Industry*. Boston: Charles River Associates.

Winner, Langdon. 1986. *The Whale and the Reactor: A Search for Limits in an Age of High Technology*. Chicago: The University of Chicago Press.

Wirth, George F., Perry W. Brunner, and Ferial S. Bishop. 1981. "Regulatory Actions." In *Stratospheric Ozone and Man*. Vol. 2. Edited by Frank A. Bower and Richard B. Ward. Boca Raton, FL: CRC Press.

World Commission on Environment and Development. 1987. *Our Common Future*. Oxford: Oxford University Press.

World Meteorological Organization, 1986. *Atmospheric Ozone 1985: Assessment of Our Understanding of the Processes Controlling its Present Distribution and Change*. Global Ozone Research and Monitoring Project, Report No. 16.

*World Resources 1992–93*. 1992. A Report by the World Resources Institute in collaboration with the United Nations Environment Programme and the United Nations Development Programme. New York: Oxford University Press.

*World Resources 1994–95*. 1994 . New York: Oxford University Press.

*World Resources 1996–97*. 1996. New York: Oxford University Press.

"World Steel Industry Warns Against Emissions Cuts." *Reuters*, 17 October, 1997.

Young, Oran R. 1989. *International Cooperation: Building Regimes for Natural Resources and the Environment*. Ithaca, NJ: Cornell University Press.

———. 1989. "The Politics of International Regime Formation: Managing Natural Resources and the Environment." *International Organization* 43, 3 (Summer):349–375.

# INDEX

adaptation
  balance with community, 111
  community and, 111
  compared to learning, 133n. 25
  complex systems, characteristic of,
    105–107
  costs of, 124n. 22
  in disorder, 107
  by economy, 36
  of ideas, 3, 9, 77
  to natural goods limits, 3, 9, 36, 110
  of society, 9, 108
  of states' preferences, 133n. 25
  technology, used for, 3
agriculture, effects of, 135n. 10
alternative energy, effect of taxes on, 116
analytic uncertainty, 74
  in international system, 68
anarchy, in international system, 68
  defined, 130n. 5
animal rights, 84, 135n. 7, 136n. 17
anthropocentrism, 68
authority
  of community, 59
  environment, for protection of, 52–54
  of state, 93

beliefs
  about policy outcomes, 110
  in epistemic communities, 75–76

on non-human rights, change in, 84
  principled and causal, 73–74
beliefs and values. *See* ideas
biocentric equality, 92
biocentrism, 89–90
biodiversity, 13
bioengineering, 6, 148
biological determinism, 91
  of women, 86
bioregionalism, 84–85, 135n. 8
  deep ecology compared, 136–137n.
    20
brown growth, conservatism of, 96
Brundtland Commission
  defines sustainable development, 2
  in equity narrative, 6
  international equity, required, 71
  international institutions' effects,
    115
  international institutions needed,
    78–79

capital, natural, human, physical, 33–
    34
civilization
  environment, separate from, 83, 107
  order, hierarchy, in 120n. 8
climate change, 29, 35, 173
  adaptation and mitigation costs, 27,
    124n. 22

165

environmentalism
    anthropocentrism of, 81, 134n. 3
    defined, 81–82
    ecologism compared, 7, 81–82, 96,
        134n. 2, 134n. 3
environmental non-government
        organizations
    in civil society, 78
    community, collective action, and,
        80
    economics of, 122n. 7
    political influence of, 96, 117–118,
        133n. 27, 133n. 28, 133n. 29
    public awareness, influence on, 23,
        78, 94, 137n. 25
environmental management, 81, 134n.
        3
environmental problems
    global and local, causes and effects,
        68–70, 130n. 7
    interaction, 13–14
environmental technology, benefits of,
        127n. 19
epistemic communities, 75–76, 79
equity
    between generations, 6
    Bruntland Commission on, 2–3, 6
    international, 67, 71
    justice, fairness, 127–128n. 2, 128n.
        3
equity policy narrative, premises,
        logic of, 6–7, 51
ethics
    engineering and, 44–45
    international relations, 129–130n. 3
    morals compared, 84, 134n. 5
    in politics, 63
    property rights and, 54–55, 89
evolutionary economics, 36, 42–43
experts
    combining opinions of, 17
    epistemic community, members of,
        75
    guesses of, 14
    influence of, 76, 137n. 22
    objective decisions by, 52

externalities, 27, 123n. 18
Exxon Valdez, 24

feedbacks, 45–46, 109
female/male roles, 86–87, 135n. 9,
        135n. 10
feminism, 128n. 6
fertilizer, losses of, 14
fisheries, 13, 121n. 4
flexibility, of policy, 109–110
food supplies, sufficiency, 12
free-riding, 128n. 5

Gaia, 89–90
German green party, 137n. 24
global atmosphere, 12–13, 69–70
global civil society, 78–79, 80
global environmental problems, 68–
        70, 130n. 7
global governance, 68
globalization, 115, 138n. 9
global market, 70
    LDCs, effect on, 67, 129n. 1
global structures, effects of, 70–71
global warming and cooling, 12–13
government
    in communitarianism, 59
    defined, 51–52
    intervention in markets, 24–25, 27–
        28, 124n. 29
    in liberalism, 57–58
    mitigating inequities, 55
    professionals, educated by, 48
    scientific research, funding by, 49–
        50, 116
green auditing, 11, 139n. 11
green political parties, 128n. 4
    ecologism and, 137n. 24
green theories. See ecologism
green theory of value, 95
gross domestic/national product and
        waste, pollution, 24

hegemony, 93–94
historical materialism, 129n. 1, 132n.
        21

# DATE DUE

| | | | |
|---|---|---|---|
| | | | |
| | | | |
| | | | |
| | | | |
| | | | |
| | | | |
| | | | |
| | | | |
| | | | |
| | | | |
| | | | |
| | | | |
| | | | |
| | | | |
| | | | |
| | | | |
| | | | |
| | | | |
| | | | |
| | | | |
| | | | Printed in USA |

HIGHSMITH #45230